# Critical Thinking Now

# Critical Thinking Now

## Practical Teaching Methods for Classrooms around the World

Nancy Burkhalter

ROWMAN & LITTLEFIELD
Lanham • Boulder • New York • London

Published by Rowman & Littlefield
A wholly owned subsidiary of The Rowman & Littlefield Publishing Group, Inc.
4501 Forbes Boulevard, Suite 200, Lanham, Maryland 20706
www.rowman.com

Unit A, Whitacre Mews, 26-34 Stannary Street, London SE11 4AB

British Library Cataloguing in Publication Information Available

**Library of Congress Cataloging-in-Publication Data Available**

ISBN 978-1-4758-2750-7 (cloth : alk. paper)
ISBN 978-1-4758-2751-4 (pbk. : alk. paper)
ISBN 978-1-4758-2753-8 (electronic)

♾™ The paper used in this publication meets the minimum requirements of American National Standard for Information Sciences—Permanence of Paper for Printed Library Materials, ANSI/NISO Z39.48-1992.

Printed in the United States of America

*To Vera John-Steiner, who has profoundly shaped my thinking on literacy, cognition, and society. I can only hope to inspire my students half as much as you have inspired me.*

# Contents

# List of Illustrations

## FIGURES

## TABLES

# Foreword

I met Nancy Burkhalter in 2011, when I interviewed her for the English Language Fellows program. This is a U.S. State Department program, similar to a Fulbright, for English language professionals. During our short conversation, her insights about teaching and the range and depth of her ideas impressed me. Our conversation stayed with me. Fast-forward 18 months: When my department was looking for an instructor to teach an intensive program for incoming international graduate students, I immediately thought of Nancy. She had recently completed her fellowship and accepted the position.

It's an extremely demanding course: Five hours a day of teaching high-level academic skills. I also taught the course and, as we worked together closely, I grew to greatly admire and respect Nancy. It didn't surprise me at all when I learned she was working on a book about teaching critical thinking. When she asked me to read the manuscript, I jumped at the chance. It's the book you don't know that you need, but once you start reading, you realize you can't do without it.

An ESL teacher for 17 years, I currently teach intermediate and advanced reading and composition in the International and English Language Programs at the University of Washington. In our department, we spend a considerable amount of time trying to improve our program. This requires ongoing effort to fine-tune our curriculum and align course outcomes to assessment. And always there is discussion of critical thinking. Our last curriculum committee meeting focused on our advanced writing courses. For the next meeting, the facilitator asked me to prepare answers to these questions: What do we mean by critical thinking? What are our students learning in our classes? What should critical thinking look like? How can we improve what we are doing?

Luckily, I had just finished the book you are about to read. This allowed me to respond in a focused, specific way. Thanks to what I learned, I could report that critical thinking *is* happening in my classroom. But thanks to the strategies and activities that Nancy suggests, I realized that I could do even more. Here are a few ways that this book transformed my teaching.

First, it helped me plan my lessons. I found it easy to modify the exercises Nancy suggests to suit the research class that I regularly teach. I've added more reflective writing about the argument paper I routinely assign. I also had students write counter argument dialogs and act them out in front of the class. This led to revisions, which eventually were incorporated into their papers. A difficult task, therefore, became relatively painless and surprisingly rewarding.

In addition to their research papers, my students read *The Hunger Games*, and I leveraged quite a few of Nancy's exercises. Questions based on Bloom's Taxonomy created lively and thoughtful discussions. I also adapted the ranking exercise she mentions in chapter 3 to apply to themes in the novel, which led to high levels of motivation and participation. This all came together in a project-based mock trail at the end of the quarter.

On the day of the trial, I didn't know what to expect. But all we had been working toward all quarter—a certain level of competence in analyzing and creating arguments, and persuading an audience—paid off. The jury found they had real issues to consider and serious deliberations to undertake.

*Critical Thinking Now* also inspired me to get rid of activities and exercises that did not belong in a critical thinking classroom: Multiple-choice tests and true/false questions. No one missed them. Short-answer responses are surprisingly simple to evaluate, especially as students grow more adept at writing them.

Nancy argues that in a critical classroom, the teacher must let go of the idea that he or she is the main provider of information. As an experienced teacher, I knew this, but as I began to seriously consider my role in the classroom, I made a conscious effort to relinquish authority and control. I turned the research process into more of an inquiry process. At one point, a student chose a topic that I was worried would not work. We talked about my reservations, but I quickly sensed how invested she was in the topic. I finally agreed and said, "Go for it!" As soon as I said this, a light suddenly appeared in her eyes. Overall, I sensed that my students appreciated how I gave them the opportunity to think for themselves.

Finally, the book helped me to respond more quickly and effectively to writing that did not hit the mark. In chapter 2, I found an extremely useful chart that identifies what critical thinking is and is not. According to the chart, critical thinking is clear, accurate, precise, relevant, deep, broad, logical, significant, and fair. I gave this chart to students, and we found examples of each in our class readings. I then created examples that broke these rules so they could see the difference.

Once students understood these standards, I could pinpoint where their own writing might improve. After years of teaching composition, I learned something new and valuable about how to break writing down into manageable chunks for both the students and the teacher.

It's not often that I find a book that dramatically informs and improves my teaching. In a clear, accessible way, *Critical Thinking Now* guides me toward creating a classroom where ideas can thrive. Although making these changes is challenging at times, they made it extremely rewarding to teach my course. I'm looking forward to using this book again and again.

Michelle Foshee
Lecturer
International and English Language Programs
University of Washington

# Preface

## *Why I Wrote This Book*

I used to run into strong headwinds when teaching critical thinking. Progress seemed painfully slow, with many students giving me blank stares, furrowed brows, and exasperated sighs. I now know that these reactions arose partly from my not understanding how to teach students to think critically and partly from not appreciating who I was teaching.

I looked high and low for a book—*one* book—that would tell me how to untangle this mess. Surely someone had written the bible on critical thinking for the rest of us. In fact, I found a thicket of information, but each source limited its focus to one or two aspects: Its definition, some exercises, formal and informal logic, and so on. Unfortunately, none told me how to analyze *why* students were having problems learning how to think critically. And missing in action was any discussion of how to teach it to second-language learners. So, I was left to blaze my own path.

After much research and years of using my own classroom as a crucible, I have cobbled together answers in this one book for you—the educator, the entrepreneur, the curriculum designer, and test maker—anyone who teaches a subject requiring the weighing of arguments, problem-solving, and logical reasoning. By my estimation, this means the discussion applies to all fields and educators, whether you teach language arts or constitutional law.

My inquiry into critical thinking began as a doctoral student in educational linguistics at the University of New Mexico. I wanted to find out more about how higher-level thinking and writing interacted. I turned my attention to persuasive essays because they require very clear, focused, and well-developed support, the same elements involved in critical thinking. Interestingly, I discovered that the very act of writing in this genre actually improves critical thinking precisely because of the demands it makes on higher-order thinking skills. It's a kind of mental bootstrapping that lays the groundwork for future learning.

So, imagine my surprise when I found out that persuasive writing was rarely taught before high school, ostensibly, according to some child development experts, because younger pupils are not cognitively mature enough to muster the challenging abstract thought that is necessary to pull it off. Yet, other researchers say all learning in children is possible provided they are given enough support.

This ability to put forth cogent, convincing oral arguments came as no surprise to many parents of nine- and ten-year-olds in the study. They all said unreservedly, "My kid? Argue? No problem!" So, why can't they learn to formulate those thoughts in writing and enrich their critical thinking in the process? Moreover, I reasoned, if we held off the teaching of this genre until later in students' education, weren't we missing out on a grand opportunity to develop their higher-level thinking skills?

To test my theory, I designed a three-week unit for two 4th- and two 6th-grade teachers on how to write a persuasive essay (See Appendix 1 for the curriculum). I hypothesized that the younger students could demonstrate the ability to write cogent, well-supported arguments, provided they receive adult guidance. The unit was designed to lean on their highly developed oral skills through discussions and debates before they wrote their essays.

Results showed that the 4th graders did just as well as the more cognitively mature 6th graders in creating and justifying their arguments in writing. So, as far as my research was concerned, persuasive essays were fair game for writers as young as nine, who would also be better off for the effort.

This was the first piece of the puzzle that I found out about critical thinking: Kids this age could learn to critically think through writing. But then I began teaching international students. I naively thought all learners were created equal. It shouldn't matter if they came from the United States, Uruguay, or Uganda as to how easily they can learn critical thinking, right?

Boy, was I wrong. Most struggled mightily. At first, I blamed their underdeveloped language skills that might be hindering expression of complex ideas. This theory was blown to smithereens when I saw it held true even for many fluent English language learners. Yes, they were grappling with a new rhetorical pattern (and in a second language to boot). But even after weeks of instruction, most wrote superficial, poorly organized, and inadequately supported essays, much more slowly than their native-speaking counterparts.

After more research and experimentation, I considered this possibility: If learners hailed from an educational background emphasizing memorization and regurgitation, they might not have sufficient cognitive readiness to deal with tasks involving critical thinking. (Notice I said readiness, *not* capability.)

Apparently, my theory about teaching critical thinking now had to take into account a student's schooling, too. Somehow this background meant students had different pathways for learning. We in the West grew up being asked open-ended questions and defending our positions. Their way of being educated had created other kinds of grooves for acquiring knowledge. So, I concluded, coaxing them out of those habitual furrows and helping them create new ones for critical thinking was the task at hand. Things were getting complicated.

In 2008, I moved abroad to train teachers in post-Soviet Kazakhstan, Russia, Ukraine, and Kosovo. Many were master's students seeking training in new methods for teaching English. Soon there arrived another snag: Some seemed suspicious and even hostile. They argued about why they should adopt these ideas when theirs had worked so well. Others simply shut me out. What could cause such unusually strong resistance? Headwinds ahoy!

Perplexed by this strong and emotional pushback, I set about studying the history of the Soviet and post-Soviet educational system. I also circulated questionnaires and conducted interviews to better understand this curious reaction. All the evidence pointed to very unsparing treatment during their schooling and work life, including public shaming for not knowing the answer and swift retribution for violating protocols and policies.

Such severe practices can result in what psychologists call "the authoritarian personality." This theory holds that certain kinds of punitive treatment cause some people to narrow their cognition and even become closed off to new information. Such a phenomenon can occur in any culture where young people undergo harsh treatment from a controlling authority figure.

These revelations led to my current theory about the hurdles to teaching critical thinking to international students:

1. Limited language abilities can usurp higher-order thinking.
2. Well-rehearsed learning patterns of memorization and regurgitation can affect cognitive readiness.
3. Learning under fear can throw up roadblocks to future learning.

In short, both education *and* culture inform a person's cognition. This realization—and the theme of this book—has forever changed the way I approach teaching.

My understanding of critical thinking has unfurled slowly over the decades. I've attended and presented at conferences, given workshops, designed curricula and exercises, and written my fair share about the topic, culminating in this book. I find the teaching of critical thinking to be invigorating and engaging for both teacher and student, but it can also be frustrating. I hope my ideas help you accomplish the former and minimize the latter. Your mission is clear: To teach this process, regardless of your students' language, culture, or habits of learning.

Teachers, this book's for you.

# Acknowledgments

Many thanks to those who provided invaluable feedback: John C. Bean, Consulting Professor of Writing and Assessment at Seattle University; Enoch Hale, Learning Innovation Consultant of Academic Learning Transformation Lab at Virginia Commonwealth University and former faculty member at the Foundation for Critical Thinking; and Michelle Foshee, a veteran ESL instructor in the International English Language Programs at the University of Washington and an English Language Fellow posted in Kosovo under the aegis of the U.S. Department of State. Each has a stake in fostering critical thinking and contributed unique insights and keen observations.

I am indebted to the wonderful teachers and faculty in Kazakhstan, Russia, and Kosovo, who unstintingly contributed to my knowledge of critical thinking.

Alexander Kubacki deserves a round of applause for reconstructing his favorite question from a college botany exam, for his own fierce critical thinking skills, and for his much-needed support in my efforts. Yes, son, as you so wisely counseled, I have finally let this book fly away.

I am eternally grateful to Steve Kubacki for helping me thrust and parry with those mad demons who colluded time and again to strangle my muses. Touché!

# Introduction

This book is about teaching and learning critical thinking. To that end, it shows how to create exercises and conduct assessments. It seeks to help anyone wanting to incorporate higher-level thinking skills into any curriculum, from topics as diverse as banking to podiatry. This may seem like a pretty broad swath of people needing to know how to teach critical thinking, but it is easily dwarfed by the galactically large number of people needing to learn it.

This book does not intend to cover chapter and verse about critical thinking; the issues are too wide ranging and addressed in greater detail elsewhere. Rather, it provides a framework to help discriminate between and among the different cognitive activities involved in critical thinking. That discussion broadens out to unexplored territory about how to teach it to foreign students on your soil or theirs.

Chapter 1 provides a brief overview of how and why critical thinking arose in the West as well as how different cultures learn and perceive the world. Chapter 2 discusses the general issues about critical thinking, such as its definition, and introduces information about how to teach it, regardless of who your students are. In chapter 3, several methods for teaching critical thinking are provided along with exemplars of exercises that can be tailored to your audience's needs. Chapter 4 looks at assessment techniques for written and oral work.

Chapter 5 spotlights students from non-Western educational systems and cultures who may also speak a different first language. The research, which draws on data and experiences from several overseas posts, can help you bridge barriers and avoid unexpected pitfalls when teaching these populations.

The epilogue presents some final observations about the field of critical thinking.

The first appendix includes the entire three-week curriculum for a 4th- and 6th-grade unit for teaching critical thinking and persuasive writing; Appendix 2 presents a table of the various verbs associated with the six categories under Bloom's Taxonomy; and Appendix 3 provides the assignment and grid for a workshop about choosing volunteers to create a colony on the moon.

Last, the annotated resources evaluate 18 books, articles, websites, and institutions. Not all of these items are cited in this text but have been included here because of their unusually important and practical contribution to the teaching and learning of critical thinking. Doubtless, there are many others that have been inadvertently overlooked.

*Chapter 1*

# How Culture Colors Cognition

This book is, first and foremost, about critical thinking: What it is, how we teach it, and how students learn it. But it is also about a cognitive division between the West and any non-Western culture, and what that partition means for teaching international students in your home country or theirs. What barriers can you expect to meet? How can you dismantle them? The answers may surprise you.

According to experts such as Richard Nisbett (*Geography of Thought,* 2003), a bright line is drawn between Far Eastern and Western thought processes. Critical thinking is, after all, a phenomenon shaped first by Socrates, and then by his students, Plato, and especially Aristotle, who lit the path for what would become the scientific method. In contrast, Eastern thought stems from the philosophy of Confucianism, which emphasizes harmony. These two vastly different ways of approaching the world have enormous implications for not only *what* students learn but *how* we teach them as well.

Nisbett explains that Greece provided a fertile environment for the development of critical thinking because of its prolific trade. Such vigorous commerce with far-flung cultures required a way to deal with conflicts arising from different trade practices, religions, and personalities. China, Korea, and Japan, on the other hand, were heavily influenced by Confucianism's ultimate aim of reaching a compromise. Even if there were disputes, the goal was always to reduce hostility and return to that state of harmony.

This Asian ideal was important for an agrarian society, whose farmers were largely isolated and depended a great deal on one another, thus foregrounding the importance of getting along. Confucianism also taught that the upper class needed to be educated in the classics to prepare them for ruling the country or region and understanding morality. The peasants, in contrast, never dealt with problems of state or anything apart from their culture and religion. They relied on the so-called gentlemen of the ruling class for guidance and so never needed to know the "why" of anything. Since Confucianism called for unity and consonance, the resultant culture had little incentive to learn how to construct an argument or analyze someone else's.

Unfortunately, a few prominent Athenians underwent some Socratic grilling and were made to feel quite foolish. Retaliation was swift: Socrates was charged with corrupting the minds of the youth and leading the hoi polloi to question their leaders. After a famous court case, the 70-year-old philosopher was condemned to death and given a fatal brew of hemlock in 399 BC to silence him once and for all.

But Socrates' method of asking targeted, piercing, unsettling questions lives on, most notably as a mainstay of law school training. He is the giant on whose shoulders many an attorney—and any critical thinker—stands today.

During the Enlightenment of the seventeenth and eighteenth centuries, modern science blossomed and with it, the development of the scientific method. Dead, or severely imperiled, were the dogmatic beliefs of theologians that had to give way to the rigors of scientific thinking. Ideally, scientists ignore emotions and consider all points of view when developing a hypothesis, analyzing the data, and drawing conclusions, all of which must be based on sound evidence and without bias.

While not all academic fields use empirical, quantitative methods to conduct experiments—some use qualitative techniques requiring copious observations, interviews, and so forth—each has its own rules for drawing conclusions, but all require rigorous data collection practices. Is it any coincidence that this kind of experimentation originated in the West or that an outsized number of Nobel Prize winners in science have come from Western countries? Hardly, concludes Nisbett. The scientific method has been neither widely accepted nor practiced in the Far East.

Other examples of these differences between Eastern and Western thinking abound. Take, for instance, the way Chinese and Western medicine approach illness. Whereas traditional medicine in the Far East seeks to maintain harmony and restore balance among all bodily functions, Western doctors see separate anatomical structures, specializing in the heart or brain, or perhaps the endocrine or urinary system. If there is a diseased organ, out it comes. Traditional Chinese medicine (until recently) is loath to target any particular organ as the problem but favors removing a blockage of the "chi" or energy flow.

The Eastern and Western ways of approaching bodily systems is but one example of how culture shapes understanding of and approaches to the world, and profoundly so, according to many evolutionary psychologists and cognitive scientists. Nisbett's book deals with how these differences play out in each culture's spatial perception and even language acquisition. For example, he says that Western infants learn nouns more quickly than verbs, and vice versa in the East.

He lists other key findings from several experiments showing that culture shapes cognition: "Habits of organizing the world, with Westerners preferring categories (e.g., taxonomy) and Easterners being more likely to emphasize relationships among items" (p. 45).

In one experiment, Nisbett showed American and Chinese children a picture of a cow and asked which item, a chicken or grass, they would associate with the cow. Because of their preference for grouping items according to relationships, the Chinese children paired the cow with the grass, because that is what it eats and what it is surrounded by outside. Westerners would most likely pair the cow and the chicken together because they are classified as animals.

The same results accrued with two other groups in a similar experiment: the Americans paired monkey with panda, while the Chinese and Taiwanese paired monkey with banana. To the Eastern mind, context, not hierarchy, governed their choice.

For those of you teaching academic writing or some other hierarchical Western analytical subject, this difference alone is enough to stymie your efforts abroad because academic/scientific writing depends on a very linear rhetorical form: Thesis statement/hypothesis, evidence, counterarguments, and conclusions. Nisbett concurs: "For my own Asian students, I find that the linear rhetorical form is the last crucial thing they learn on their road to becoming fully functioning social scientists" (p. 196).

Yet another central difference derives from the Western habit of favoring one side of an argument, whereas Easterners lean toward compromise. Here is how Nisbett contrasts the Western and Eastern approaches to dealing with arguments:

Application of dialectical approaches, with Westerners being more inclined to insist on the correctness of one belief over another and Easterners being more likely to seek the Middle Way (i.e., avoiding extremes) when confronted with apparent contradiction and Westerners being more inclined to insist on the correctness of one belief vs. another. (p. 45)

Again, Far Eastern-schooled writers may find it challenging to evaluate and support one opinion over another if they have been trained to seek resolution between the two sides. It must be said that all writers, regardless of their first language, need to learn this process, but non-Western-educated ones may have difficulties stemming from their culture as well as their inexperience as writers. (Please see chapter 5 for further discussion.)

Certainly, the discussion around these differences is much more nuanced and complex than what is presented here. Nisbett has written extensively about these and other issues involving human reasoning. His work deserves a thorough review to have a complete understanding of his claims and results. And surely similar studies done in the Near and Middle East, other parts of Asia, not to mention Central and South America, would provide an even wider, richer picture of the phenomena affecting cognition that Nisbett discusses.

While Nisbett's experiments reveal many fascinating differences between the Western and Eastern mind-set, his findings are not easily applied to the classroom. But his observations do allow us to generalize that not everyone thinks alike and that those differences in cognition stem from one's culture.

What elements in a culture influence cognition? For starters, teaching methods play a crucial role because they determine what you learn, how you learn, and how you expect to be taught in the future. Take memorization, for example, which has long been a staple of instruction around the world. Learning by rote teaches students to consume disparate facts. They become quite good at memorizing long passages and poems.

These habits of mind, as they are known, do not spontaneously arise but are shaped by one's schooling and culture. If memorization and regurgitation are the *only* instructional methods on the menu, then learners become adept at these skills. On the other hand, if they learn to, say, analyze and evaluate information, they will have these tools at their disposal. (Whether they are necessarily deployed in all domains of knowledge is a matter of lively discussion.)

Neither approach is superior; both must be learned. But to teach people to think critically requires a certain classroom configuration, student-centered teaching, and particular instructional and assessment methods (outlined in chapter 2). It also takes practice for students and teachers alike, and lots of it.

## FACTS FIRST, AND *THEN* CRITICAL THINKING?

Many teachers believe that memorization of facts and critical thinking are necessarily sequential activities and that no critical thinking can be done unless there is a critical mass of facts stored up. But this defeats the purpose of critical thinking because information should be examined *by means of* critical thinking. No fact floats around in a vacuum. All are moored to some context or viewpoint. Some statements are more debatable (e.g., teaching is the best profession) or less so (e.g., the moon rotates around the earth), but one has only to look at what people used to believe as immutable truth (e.g., the sun revolves around the earth) to see that views have changed, sometimes 180 degrees.

The point is this: One does not simply superimpose critical thinking on already acquired knowledge; rather, facts and information should be subjected to the rigors of critical thinking *as they are being learned.* For instance, we should ask whether any fact is:

- Verifiable,
- From a dependable source, and
- Consistent with other similar information.

Because thinking critically is a dynamic and dialectical process (i.e., by weighing contradictory views), there is no reason to see acquiring knowledge as a step that precedes critical thinking. Besides, facts—unless they are connected to our larger knowledge base—are more difficult to remember and deploy when asked to perform higher-level cognitive functions, such as analyzing or evaluating them.

Another reason memorizing facts constitutes a dead-end street is that facts are history. You can learn lots of information about black holes: How they are identified, how big they are, what force they exert on surrounding matter, what supergravity is, all of which would make you a super-duper contestant on *Jeopardy!* under that category. But unless you see the *relationships* among those facts, you will not have a firm basis from which to formulate new questions to help you see ahead.

Do you think NASA scientists looked at the moon and said, "It sure looks like it's made of green cheese" and were done with it? No. They asked, "How can we verify that? Do we need to go there to do so? How can we get there? What facts do we have right now that might disprove it's not made of green cheese?" If you can Google it, it won't stimulate critical thinking.

Students need to ask, "What should I do with these facts? How can I make them meaningful? How can I use information about going to the moon to advance our knowledge about astronomy, physics, or medicine?" Facts should never be the end-product of education because that would mean you are living in the past. And no one can afford to do that anymore.

It must be stated here that talking about East Asians as if they were one people is as absurd as saying that all people in the Americas share one culture. Moreover, all cultures, whether from the Argentina or Zimbabwe, exercise some form of critical thinking. One cannot get through the day without making reasoned decisions about clothing, politics, food, medicine, whatever. They just approach the task in different ways.

Any decision entails weighing arguments and coming to a rational conclusion. It would be ludicrous and unsupportable to suggest otherwise. But, as you will see in chapter 2 about critical thinking and its definition, when it comes to dealing with weightier and more contentious issues found in fields such as law, religion, biology, linguistics, science, philosophy, engineering, anthropology, sociology, business (every field, really), people must employ much more extended and elaborate thought processes involving questioning, logic, self-reflection, and so forth.

In sum, trying to get your point across to a group accustomed to rote learning, and perhaps with iffy language skills, presents challenges, but not insurmountable ones. Raising your awareness about the issues is the first step and the express purpose of this book. Everyone wants to learn, but not everyone is ready to learn the way *you* learn. So, if you want to be successful as a teacher, you have some critical thinking of your own to do.

## Chapter 2

# What is Critical Thinking?

## THE *WHAT* OF CRITICAL THINKING

Critical thinking is like pornography: Everyone knows it when they see it, but no one agrees on its definition. Many descriptions are ponderous, lengthy, and involved, and list traits of the critical thinker or activities associated with the act. Other definitions are terser; many overlap. (See works by Beyer, 1987; Ennis, 1962; Halpern, 1993; Lipman, 2003; Paul, 1995; and Paul and Elder, 2012, for discussions of definitions. Also, consult Moseley et al., 2005 for a much broader discussion of thinking.)

Concurrence on a definition may not happen soon. But, you need not wait for scholars to reach consensus on the fine points before getting on with instruction. You teachers are by temperament and by necessity a practical lot. Your work is all about the doing. So, let's consider one definition to get you rolling.

Here is one helpful definition that is quite elegant in its terseness: *Critical thinking is the awakening of the mind to the study of itself, or, in short, thinking about thinking.* It's from Richard Paul, the noted philosopher and writer, who has quite a lot more to say on the subject in his books and through his Foundation for Critical Thinking.

The takeaway from Paul's definition is that critical thinking is, and should be, effortful. Its goal is to prevent thoughts from flowing, unexamined, through learners' minds and directly out of their mouths. Critical thinking is a learned feedback loop to help people examine and turn their thinking back on itself to assess it, according to Paul's (or others') criteria. This process prevents minds from going on autopilot, which often leads to making ill-considered decisions about which products to buy or leaders to elect based solely on what commercials or candidates say.

This definition also points out how important it is to reflect. Critical thinking may not happen fast, but it is intentional and always involves bringing an awareness to how you come to your conclusions. In other words, it is the deliberate act of considering and reconsidering your thinking and especially those espousing views with whom you disagree. Have you thought of all the arguments? Have you weighed theirs and yours properly? Have you owned up to your assumptions and justified them? Can you articulate the other side(s) of the argument and do it as fairly and objectively as possible?

The Institute for Critical Thinking has done much to catalog many aspects of critical thinking and disseminate that information through conferences, literature, workshops, and its website. It has developed a comprehensive approach to critical thinking by delineating:

- The intellectual standards by which one assesses critical thinking,
- The elements of thought, and
- The traits of a fair-minded thinker.

These are the three legs of the stool upon which the foundation's faculty base their teachings, such as how to improve student learning, read and write a paragraph, study and learn, detect media bias, think scientifically, and so forth. There is no critical thought, Paul maintains, unless one fastidiously adheres to these standards when, say, judging material on the Internet or TV, in a newspaper or magazine, or during a discussion.

Table 2.1 presents Paul and Elder's (2012) nine standards (with their opposites added) against which you can assess your thinking.

These standards provide some good guidelines for critical thinking. But without instruction, they do not easily translate into actionable classroom activities and assessment practices, not to mention outcomes or objectives for your courses. This is what this book attempts to do in chapters 3 and 4.

Benjamin Bloom's *Taxonomy of Educational Objectives* (1956; Anderson et al., 2001) brings the discussion a bit closer to something you can build

**Table 2.1    What Critical Thinking Is, and Is Not**

| Critical thinking *is* . . . | Critical thinking *is not* . . . |
| --- | --- |
| 1. clear | muddled |
| 2. accurate | distorted or untrue |
| 3. precise | too general or lacking in detail |
| 4. relevant | off topic |
| 5. deep | superficial or obvious |
| 6. broad (perspective) | narrow- or closed-minded |
| 7. logical | contradictory, irrational, fallacious |
| 8. significant | trivial or irrelevant |
| 9. fair | one-sided, biased, unjust |

*Source*: Adapted from Paul & Elder, 2012.

a curriculum on. Bloom, along with his team of educational measurement experts, wrote a taxonomy that categorized six levels of cognition: Knowledge, comprehension, application, analysis, synthesis, and evaluation (See Figure 2.1). These levels are ordered from simple to complex, and from concrete to abstract, with the top three skills generally being associated with critical thinking.

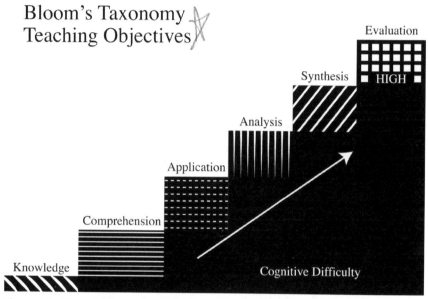

**Figure 2.1   Bloom's Taxonomy—Teaching Objectives (Bloom et al., 1956)**

Bloom originally intended for students to master each level before proceeding to the next, but in 2001, educator Lorin Anderson (a student of Bloom) and his seven colleagues revised the taxonomy, changing nouns to verbs, reasoning they would better reflect the cognitive processes, as shown in Figure 2.2. The researchers also changed *synthesis* to *create* and placed it at the top of the taxonomy. David Krathwohl (2002), who served on both teams of researchers, reports that when they revised the taxonomy, they wanted to emphasize that these cognitive processes are not rigidly separated, but overlap.

In fact, if you examine Table A2.1 in Appendix 2, you will notice that some categories share verbs: "predict," for instance, occurs under both *understand* and *apply*; "explain" occurs under *evaluate* and *create*. This double-billing shows that these levels represent different, but not necessarily discrete, mental activities. That sharing between and among these skills means that a person does not, and probably cannot, engage purely in analysis, but must employ a blend of several skills.

# Bloom's Taxonomy Teaching Objectives

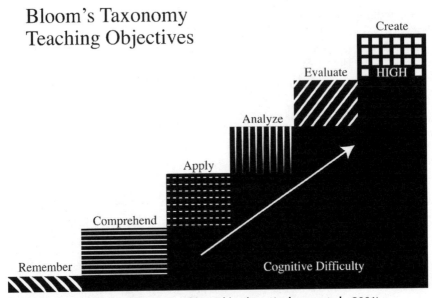

Figure 2.2   Bloom's Taxonomy—Teaching Objectives (Anderson et al., 2001)

For instance, who could analyze, say, the War of 1812 without remembering facts such as where it took place and the parties involved? Similarly, *application* subsumes *understanding* because you must comprehend the information if you are to draw a map of the United States during that war. All the steps challenge our mental faculties, just in a different way.

Because the categories overlap, it would also be a mistake to try to teach them in lockstep fashion, as Krathwohl points out. First of all, to teach to one level to the exclusion of others (even if you could) not only denies learners the opportunity to develop all their faculties, but it could also make lessons rather mechanical and boring. Moreover, learners need to employ all the skills to enrich the very knowledge they are acquiring. In the same vein, to design activities as if these processes developed sequentially oversimplifies the human mind. They are too imbricated and complicated to tease apart.

Even though these skills intersect, most experts agree that the top three—analyze, evaluate, and create—comprise the cognitive skills people draw upon when thinking critically. Research has shown that students, even those as young as nine, can think at those higher levels if given the chance and enough help from adults (Burkhalter, 1995).

What follows is a rough illustration of how to, for instance, formulate questions using Bloom's Taxonomy (the 2001 version) using "Goldilocks and the Three Bears":

Level 1: Remember

Recall information.

*Remember: Who was Goldilocks?*

Level 2: Understand

Know what is being communicated in order to make use of the information.

*Comprehend: Why is Goldilocks in danger?*

Level 3: Apply

Use a learned skill in a new situation or convert the abstract into the concrete.

*Apply: Act out this story, but make all the characters adult humans.*

Level 4: Analyze

Break down information into its integral parts and identify the relationship of each part of the total organization.

*Analyze: Explain each bear's reaction to what Goldilocks did and give examples.*

Level 5: Evaluate

Make a judgment about the value of something by using a standard.

*Evaluate: What do you think Goldilocks' mother said about her misadventure?*

Level 6: Create

The ability to combine existing elements in order to create something original.

*Create: Write a poem about Goldilocks or a letter from Goldilocks to the three bears apologizing for her behavior.*

You can see how the questions become more and more open-ended and deviate from rote learning as they go up the scale. They challenge a person's ability to think more deeply about the story and to draw conclusions not explicitly given.

This hierarchy can be used to devise various questions for a test or class discussion about more substantive topics you might study. Take a unit on dinosaurs, for instance:

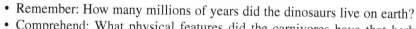

- Remember: How many millions of years did the dinosaurs live on earth?
- Comprehend: What physical features did the carnivores have that herbivores did not?
- Apply: What kinds of information can scientists infer from bones they discover?

- Analyze: Why were there so few mammals when the dinosaurs were alive?
- Evaluate: How do paleontologists know that a bone they find at a dig belongs to a dinosaur?
- Create: Some experts believe that the history of birds begins with the Archaeopteryx. Write a paper or give a presentation about what character-istics modern-day birds share with the Archaeopteryx convincing us that today's birds are/are not its descendants. (*Note to teacher:* Share your crite-ria for a well-organized, well-supported paper or presentation ahead of time.)

Before leaving the ideas of Bloom (1956) and Anderson (2001) behind, there is one more comment that needs to be made. Yes, this taxonomy has been roundly criticized for being not really representative of critical thinking per se. And, no, one does not magically sprout critical thinking dendrites if you ask someone to classify dinosaurs as carnivores or herbivores. But, paying attention to all these steps in the taxonomy means students get to prac-tice a *range* of mental activities. So, it is offered more as an awareness-raising tool rather than a prescriptive one. This is for certain: It's surely not the end of the discussion about how to become a good critical thinker.

## CAN EVERYONE LEARN TO THINK CRITICALLY? IT DEPENDS ON YOUR DISPOSITION

An interesting issue surrounding the teaching of critical thinking concerns one's temperament, also called "the affective domain" or "disposition." As with certain personal qualities that make teachers successful in the classroom, such as patience, understanding, and compassion, critical thinking demands that people have certain traits that allow them to think critically. Table 2.2 presents the eight that Paul and Elder (2012) list, along with their opposites.

These eight traits are a sort of contract people make as critical thinkers so they don't get pulled down into the seductive vortex of destructive emotions and self-centered thinking. If people try to exhibit these eight traits, it means they commit to improving their way of approaching the world. They agree that highly partisan, rash thinking is nonproductive and that others, even if they don't agree with them, still have a point worth considering.

The shouters on certain talk radio and TV shows have not taken such an oath, even if they know what it is. The people on Public Broadcasting System's *The News Hour* do observe that protocol because they discuss matters in rational, low-key ways, and resist calling the opposition names. This pledge means they can't flame out on the Internet and be intellectually humble at the same time. They can't cut people off in mid-argument and pretend to understand their point of view.

**Table 2.2    Do's and Don'ts of a Critical Thinker**

| You are a critical thinker if you show . . . | You **are not** thinking critically if you . . . |
|---|---|
| 1. Intellectual integrity. | Do not practice what you preach. |
| 2. Intellectual independence. | Do not think for yourself. |
| 3. Intellectual perseverance. | Cave into opposition and resistance from others when considering an issue. |
| 4. Intellectual empathy. | Do not put aside your beliefs to consider another's situation. |
| 5. Intellectual humility. | Claim to know more than you do. |
| 6. Intellectual courage. | Dismiss out of hand others' ideas, especially if they seem dangerous, absurd, or threatening to you. |
| 7. Confidence in reason. | Allow emotions to push out evidence and facts. |
| 8. Fair-mindedness. | Are biased. |

*Source*: Adapted from Paul & Elder, 2012.

Anonymity often emboldens people to skip the courtesy part of human interaction and allows them to hold forth in the comments section in chat rooms and websites with total disregard for the author's ideas, not to mention feelings. It's not enough to know how to be a critical thinker; people have to act like one, too. When they do, it means they leave room to change their opinion and risk expressing an unpopular one. It's not the easy route, but it is one that promotes reasoned discussion and the feeling that people have been heard and respected. This goes a long way toward achieving a civil society.

## HOW CAN WE IDENTIFY A CRITICAL THINKER?

People often ask how they can recognize critical thinkers. It's easier to identify someone who is *not* engaging in it: Anyone shouting at you; a person claiming to be right just because of who she or he is; someone who accepts the easiest solution first and refuses to consider the other side; or an individual offering a reason that is self-serving or lacks proper backing. Poor critical thinkers in a writing class are especially easy to spot because they present poorly supported, unsound, absolutist arguments that are often off-topic, ignore others' positions, and brim with assumptions and self-righteousness, sometimes all in one essay.

Part of their problem stems from their lack of good instruction in how to put forth arguments, but that poor performance may also accrue to being stuck at the lower levels of Bloom's Taxonomy: They've never learned *how* to think, which is to say, to support their ideas or put forth a reasoned point of view. Even orally, they produce shallow or irrelevant evidence to shore up their opinions, often engaging in circular thinking.

These poor habits of mind are especially prevalent when it comes to emotional topics such as abortion and gun control, when it is easiest to lose perspective and revert to personal attacks and, at times, religious arguments. (*Note*: Religious arguments are not valid pieces of support in academia since not all readers might believe in the source cited.) Logic is instantly derailed.

These emotions may originate from a fear of going against a cherished belief system or inviolable parental teachings. It may also mean validating views that have been anathema to them perhaps since birth. Doing this is hard for anyone. But, if the people are considering the welfare of everyone involved, then they will need to judge the evidence more impartially.

It's easy to dismiss people who don't agree with you as poor critical thinkers. They may be. But it will be more productive to analyze *why* you perceive that deficit. In the end, it is more important how you respond to them, because only then will they feel they have been heard, open their minds to other ideas, and join you in reaching a consensus.


## CONCLUSION

Of the myriad definitions of critical thinking, the simplest one may be the best guide: Critical thinking occurs when you think about your thinking. This skill of examining your judgments and beliefs is aided by Paul and Elder's standards and also by Bloom's Taxonomy, which divides the range of cognitive skills into six categories, from the concrete to the abstract.

This taxonomy can help you plan your syllabus, activities, tests, and outcomes to ensure that you aim instruction at all cognitive levels, especially at the highest ones of analyzing, evaluating, and creating. Also vital to the process of critical thinking are the dispositions to remain impartial, fair-minded, patient, humble, and courageous when dealing with others. They counsel deliberate and deliberative thinking. The next time you have a disagreement, listen carefully to their explanation, weigh the arguments, and then be sure to assess your own. Only then will you have a solid position from which to make a final decision.

Enough dilly-dallying over definitions. Let the teaching begin!

*Chapter 3*

# The Critical Thinking Classroom

In chapter 2, it was established that to critically think, one must hone the skills of analyzing, evaluating, and creating (aka synthesizing in Bloom's original 1956 taxonomy). However, one issue rarely discussed is the connection between *learning* to critically think and *teaching* people how to do it. Certainly, books exist, but they don't always give enough details or practical suggestions to help all professionals move forward. This chapter spells out how to set the stage for critical thinking and then practice it with exercises and activities.

Let's first look at who might benefit from instruction in critical thinking. Do you teach people who evaluate or analyze the following topics?

- Policies
- Results of an experiment or study
- Proposals
- Job performance
- Evidence
- Programs
- Curricula

If so, then you could profit from this chapter.

When it comes to critical thinking, there are three principal elements:

1. A classroom configuration that facilitates pair/group work,
2. A student-centered teacher, and
3. Activities that nurture critical thinking.

What do all these changes mean, exactly? Here is what they do *not* mean:

- Desks bolted to the floor so they face the teacher like soldiers in a dress parade,
- Endless lecturing,
- Kill-and-drill exercises, and
- Multiple choice or true–false tests.

They do mean a classroom that

- Accommodates collaboration,
- Focuses on the students, and
- Provides activities that engage, challenge, and pique learners' interest.

Caution: These elements are nonnegotiable (Burkhalter, 2013). They are all of a piece and ignored at the peril of the effectiveness of your instruction. Now, on to the details of how all of these factors play their part in the learning process.

## COMPONENTS

### Classroom Configuration

The first component in creating a critical thinking classroom may involve moving the furniture so everyone can collaborate on assignments. Arrangements should accommodate two to five people. Teamwork can be a powerful catalyst in learning. Consider the following experiment (Burkhalter, 1995) that used collaboration to help elementary kids write a persuasive essay on whether children or parents should decide which school they attend.

Since persuasive writing is a demanding genre in terms of higher-order thinking, some scholars believe that writers younger than 11 years old cannot accomplish the task because they have not yet acquired the necessary abstract reasoning skills. Other researchers say younger pupils can learn anything; it just takes proper guidance from an adult (or proficient peer). This study hypothesized that 4th and 6th graders could manage writing a well-supported, coherent persuasive essay, but only if they were first able to build on their oral skills through collaboration and debate. (See Appendix 1 for the three-week curriculum.) Only then would they be asked to write the essay.

To prepare for the debate, teachers arranged the desks so four pupils could collaborate. And collaborate they did! Students were leaning over one another's books, pointing, drawing, discussing, gesticulating, laughing, and yes, some were even writing. What could possibly be getting done with all this chaos? The teachers explained that this method would help young learners emerge with these benefits:

- Writers could pool and build on each other's ideas.
- They could verbalize/externalize their thinking.
- Weaker writers could learn information and strategies from the more capable thinkers in their group.
- All were empowered by having the responsibility of finding a solution.
- It was fun!

Collaboration can catalyze their thinking and is an excellent way to share their ideas. That said, on occasion, you might want to give them time alone to collect their thoughts before airing them to peers, especially when it involves analysis or evaluation. What follows is an example of a workshop that shows how private thinking, followed by collaboration with a small group of peers, can work. Only then do they publish their thoughts to the class and ultimately in writing.

The problem concerns a race among various countries to colonize the moon. The government is sending a team of four volunteers to prepare the site for future missions. Participants must decide whom to send. The four-part workshop, titled "To the Moon! A Launch Pad for Encouraging Reluctant Students to Express Their Opinions" (Burkhalter, 2011), is designed to gently lure everyone into the scary world of writing well-reasoned persuasive essays by, again, depending on oral skills and collaboration first (See Appendix 3 for the assignment and worksheets), but by first thinking for themselves.

Step 1: Review what they know about the moon and perhaps have them do preliminary research.

Step 2: Create a list of the qualities workshop participants would look for in a person joining a team going to the moon.

Step 3: Hand out the assignment along with the sheet of ten short bios and grid to explain their choices for selecting or rejecting a candidate. The age, profession, and a few personal facts are provided, such as whether they have children, and a skill or achievement that may or may not be pertinent to the situation. They must fill out the grid *by themselves* first. This step is important so they can defend their selections at the next stage.

Step 4: Ask groups of three or four to reach a consensus. Some, perhaps all, will change their minds. But in defending their reasoning, group mates must support their choices with evidence, much as they will be doing, alone, in their persuasive paper.

Step 5: Tally the groups' choices on the board as each group reports out. Teams may want to discuss any organizing principle they used (e.g., did they choose people under 40 because they would more likely to survive the journey or perhaps because of their ability to solve problems, etc.). Why were certain people not selected by anyone? What criteria did they use to exclude them? Who would they choose if they could select a fifth person? Which one would you select as captain?

In short, the steps of the workshop ask them to:

• Choose volunteers according to their own values and organizing principle,
• Back up their opinions,
• Defend their reasoning,
• Evaluate others' arguments, and
• Reevaluate their own choices to achieve consensus.

Some students can be quite timid about expressing their opinions, so this format lets them practice with little risk. Without knowing it (i.e., by being engaged in the process), workshop participants use higher-order thinking skills, such as evaluation and analysis, which are used in future exercises involving more difficult content. This workshop shows them they have every ability to do that. But they also see how important collaboration is in helping them arrive at a much more closely considered decision.

There is an additional boon to this exercise. In chapter 2, the necessary dispositions for critical thinking were outlined. It's not enough, according to Paul and Elder (2012), merely to evaluate an argument, but one must also have a particular temperament to engage in critical thinking, whether it be alone or when collaborating. These are the dispositions again, along with an explanation of why this kind of exercise calls upon them.

• Intellectual independence. Participants are given the opportunity to come to their own conclusions first. By exercising this trait, people commit to thinking for themselves and gain command over their thought processes. It is an important step, since, as critical thinking expert David Klooster (2001) puts it, "No one can critically think for you" (p. 37).
• Fair-mindedness. Participants must commit to being impartial in the face of their own beliefs and values: Should I opt for someone younger in favor of an individual who is somewhat disabled but can repair the ship if necessary? Should the 20-year-old scout stay home with elderly, sick parents? Do I choose someone with young kids? These values come into conflict when weighing all the attributes.
• Intellectual empathy. This quality demands that people imagine being in the place of others to genuinely understand them. Asking these groups to collaborate and come to a consensus forces them to see others' points of view and reevaluate their thinking.
• Intellectual courage. Individuals must be willing to hear others out and not jump to conclusions even though, at first, they might strongly object. On

the one hand, Paul (1995) points out, "It takes courage to be true to our own thinking" but on the other hand, "examining cherished beliefs is difficult, and the penalties for non-conformity are often severe" (p. 534). Once participants' ideas are subjected to the group's counterarguments, they must have the courage to defend their point of view but also the courage to admit they have changed their mind.

Additionally, this workshop shows learners that reasoned consideration takes time, and, as the third part demonstrates, cooperation has its advantages because they may not have thought of every angle. But it can also introduce the notion of making assumptions. Past participants have overwhelmingly referred to the scout as "he." Yet there is no reference to gender in the bios. Pointing this out lays the groundwork for future discussions about assumptions made in writing and speaking.

Because this exercise does not include any academic information, it lessens their cognitive burden. For instance, it would be much harder to ask them to decide which general, William T. Sherman or Robert E. Lee, fought more bravely in the Civil War unless they had studied about it.

After participating in this exercise, they are now versed in the facts and their own opinions, which can increase fluency in related writing tasks, such as a:

- Letter to one of the people not chosen, explaining their reasoning,
- Letter of congratulations to the team members, letting them know why you chose them and what you expect the mission to accomplish,
- Speech to government officials about their decisions,
- Newspaper article announcing the selection of the team members,
- Report to NASA outlining their recommendations about who was and was not chosen, and
- Letter from one of the newly selected team members informing a friend or former teacher about the honor.

These assignments help writers compose an essay from different points of view, in various genres, and to different audiences. They can also practice manipulating tone and vocabulary.

The next step is to extend the information they have already considered to several exercises with more academic content and challenges.

- Doing historical research. Classes could investigate what it was like for any of the famous explorers to prepare for their trips to the New World, the North and South Pole, etc. What were the conditions the explorers faced both on the voyage to the new destination and at the site? What skills and knowledge would a team need to overcome those challenges?

This assignment gives them practice in conducting research for a special purpose, thinking through the problems facing the group, and designing their own dream team to carry out their mission. This is an excellent first step in the direction of developing critical thinking because they must put forth their explanations and support them.

- Writing reflections. Students could reflect on topics such as how their reasoning differed from that of other group members. Which of those ideas did they accept? Were they able to change any minds about their choice and if so how? How might they restructure or rephrase any of their original arguments in order to make a stronger case? How did their group come to an "agreement" about the choices? Did they feel (un)comfortable with their group's choices? Did they get angry during negotiations? In what ways have their assumptions about space travel changed as a result of this exercise?

Finally, you could extend this exercise to the very real-life possibility of organ transplantation by having them rank-order the rules for potential recipients. They could start by formulating their own questions. For instance,

- What age should be the cutoff for a recipient?
- Should we exclude transplant applicants who are alcoholics?
- Should the fame or notoriety of the person be important?
- Should it matter if a person has had a previous transplant that didn't work out?
- Should a person jump to the head of the list because she or he can pay more for the procedure or is famous? If so, how much more?

They then sort these criteria by importance.

In the end, this kind of workshop alerts them to the need to justify their choices, better preparing them for the rigors and expectations of academic work and giving them experience with collaboration, whose benefits are discussed in more detail next. (*Note:* Some cultures and countries do not allow organ donations.)

## Constructivist Learning: Building Your Own House of Knowledge

The constructivist approach to education grew out of a very influential theory from the twentieth century. Simply stated, people construct their own knowledge and understanding of the world by experiencing things and reflecting on those experiences. Knowledge is not constructed from anything someone tells you to think. The point is made quite starkly when talking about a physical skill. If someone tells you how to ride a bike, for example, and you can parrot back all that information, do you actually *know* how to ride one? To accomplish this, you need to experience it. Unless you construct the knowledge yourself, it is not yours to manipulate in other circumstances.

## Teacher's Role

Second on the list of mandatory components is your role as instructor. You can be a teacher of anything in the world—psychiatry, film studies, rock climbing—and this information will pertain to you. By using these methods, the teacher goes from a know-it-all who holds the keys to the Magic Kingdom of Knowledge to an on-the-sidelines facilitator who helps others construct their own knowledge.

Teaching from the constructivist point of view means the classroom must be student centered. Gone are the lectures, didactic lessons, emphasis on content only, and, above all, rote learning. Facts are necessary and must be marshaled for critical thinking to occur, but a fact learned is *not* knowledge earned.

Those facts must be put into a meaningful context, not consumed through, as Richard Paul (1995) calls it, the "mother robin approach," where she places worms into the gaping maws of her baby birds, who swallow them whole. Brazilian educator Paulo Freire (2000) termed that same idea "knowledge banking," echoing the idea that memorizing facts leads to Nowheresville.

Your job is to design activities that allow students to construct their own knowledge by letting them:

• Pool knowledge,
• Contribute to discussions,
• Rely on one another to find solutions to problems,
• Ask questions,
• Create their own projects, and
• Reflect on their thinking.

All in all, anything that sends students on their way to discovering without you will do. Don't worry; you won't be out of a job: You just take on another very active role. Whereas before you were on stage most of the class time, now you will be:

• Observing,
• Taking notes,
• Helping certain individuals,
• Monitoring their progress, and
• Asking questions instead of doling out answers.

You will at no time be holding forth about this theory or that practice unless it is necessary to get them on their way to making that knowledge their own. Lecturing deadens the mind and says, *I know best. I know how you learn. I know what you need to learn. I don't care what you think.*

Instead, your mission is to provide opportunities for them to practice critical thinking. Generally, it's best to limit teacher talk to under ten minutes and then set up an exercise for them to explore that knowledge or idea. This goes for pupils of all ages. In the main, you will be using student-generated ideas as classroom material and discussions. Building on learners' interests not only chums the waters for critical thinking, it also empowers and motivates them.

You will be encouraging debate, reflection, group work, interactive games, and so forth (See books by John Bean, 2011, and Alan Crawford et al., 2005, for more excellent ideas). Such activities oblige teachers to relinquish their monopoly on power.

Surrendering control can be uncomfortable, even intolerable, to someone whose teaching philosophy is geared toward knowledge accumulation. Socrates did the exact opposite of telling his acolytes what to think. Instead, he devised a system designed to lead them to much more reasoned conclusions. He asked question after question to help them get at fundamental truths. Most important, *they* did the work, *they* grappled with the inconsistencies in their thinking, *they* dug deep to justify their views with convincing reasons, which is as it should be for your students too.

The message of this section is that critical thinking must be planned for and nurtured. Don't be surprised when learners resist (and sometimes resent) having to search for solutions. "Can't you just tell us the answer?" they might plead, frustrated at the slow pace and irritated at being asked to do something they don't know how to do. But, as you well know, thinking hurts. You should tell them to get used to it, because that's what a good education is. They need to learn how to drive their own brain, or someone will do it for them.

## Active Learning

The third component of a critical thinking/constructivist classroom is active learning, such as doing projects or problem-solving activities, reflecting on their learning, and collaborating with others. Then they discover facts, patterns, concepts, and principles for themselves. Learning occurs best when students actively participate and discern the significance on their own.

Take project-based learning (PBL) as an example of an exercise embodying the aims of critical thinking. Learners work together to solve a real-world problem, take a stand on an issue, make a presentation, or create something tangible. Such in-depth teamwork engages students because they share knowledge and learn from others. Here are some more facts about project-based learning:

- The project looks at real-world problems stemming from their concerns or interests.
- Students largely guide themselves in finding resources and applying information.
- Projects focus on goals and outcomes the teacher sets up. Learners can also contribute in this phase of the project (See Appendix 2 for verbs that can be used as outcomes).
- Groups decide how they will work together and what they will create.
- Participants reflect on everything, such as how well they are learning, how effective their inquiry is, how good the quality of their work is, what obstacles still exist, and how to overcome them.
- Teachers also reflect on how well they are facilitating the project and may choose to share those insights with the class.
- Groups assess their learning and use others' feedback to improve their outcome.
- The class publishes its results by communicating to an outside audience.

Students structure their inquiry around what is called a "driving question," which is not something they can look up in a web search or by visiting the library. Questions requiring them to do something work best. For example, how can we fix the homeless problem in Seattle? How can we build a garden behind our school that will attract hummingbirds and bees but keep out deer?

Here is a summary of a three-week life sciences project from Buck Institute for Education for 5th graders titled "Medical Interns." Their driving question asked how they could recommend the best treatment for a patient. Notice the active role the investigators take and how they present their results. No amount of Googling would help them accomplish all this.

In this scenario, students take on the role of medical interns who are asked to help diagnose sick patients and recommend the best treatment plan. They will learn about the various body systems, focusing in on the circulatory system, as they move through the project. Students will collaborate with a medical doctor via video chat, interview mock patients, and engage in research to reach their findings. In teams, they will present their diagnosis and recommendations to a panel of experts, parents, and classmates. (Buck Institute for Education, n.d.)

Visit the Buck Institute for Education site for more on the project design, activities, and assessments.

Projects can develop critical thinking by having participants make judgments between alternatives, determine the best way to create something, weigh evidence, reconsider initial ideas, create a plan for solving a problem, and summarize an argument's key points. PBL can take some practice to implement correctly, but its breadth of inquiry and rich opportunity for critical thinking make it well worth the effort.

So far, this chapter has provided a general overview of the approach recommended for setting up your critical thinking classroom. Collaboration, student-centered teaching, and active learning are three features for accomplishing that. But letting students discover information on their own takes patience and an entirely different role than you may be used to, and it may even be a bit scary. Some of you may reject these new methods, feeling as if you've lost control over what students are learning. But losing control and putting students in charge is, or should be, the whole idea.

In fact, you aren't really losing control. It's just been moved to another part of the learning process: Your preparation and management of their inquiry. Teachers new to this method commonly complain that it takes too much time, and many fret they won't get through all their lessons. With all due respect, if you don't give them time to learn the material, then why bother teaching it at all?

What follows are several exercises, both written and oral, to encourage critical thinking, along with some advice for both teachers and students.

## CRITICAL THINKING EXERCISES

On the premise that critical thought flourishes in a classroom set up for collaboration and taught by a teacher who promotes active learning by making students responsible for their own education, here are some activities that promote critical thinking. Far from exhaustive, this list provides only exemplars of the many exercises that nurture higher-order thinking. Authors such as Bean (2011), Crawford et al. (2005), Moon (2008), Tishman et al. (1995) and websites such as The Thinking Classroom Consortium and Buck Institute for Education offer a lot more activities. Tailor the following as you see fit.

### Questioning—A Fulcrum for Knowledge

Many people may think that getting an education is all about answering questions when it's really all about *asking* them to carry their thinking forward. Answers just stop it cold, while questions invite further investigation. So, the first step is to ask questions, but you should be mindful that not all questions are created equal. In general terms, they can be categorized by whether they employ lower-level or higher-level cognitive abilities. Look at this example from Crawford's text on teaching critical thinking:

Lower level thinking: "What temperature does water freeze at sea level?"

**versus**

Higher level thinking: "Why does water near bridges and in the cities freeze later in the winter than water in lakes located in rural areas?" (p. 5)

Here is another pair of lower-versus higher-order questions for botany students:

Lower level thinking: Describe the process of photosynthesis.

**versus**

Higher level thinking: *Euglena* is a genus of single-celled flagellate protists. This organism is unusual because it has two flagella, allowing it to move and feed on other organisms, like an animal, but it can also create its own food through photosynthesis, like a plant. How would you classify *Euglena*, as an animal or a plant, or would you classify it some other way? Defend your choice of classification. (Adapted from an advanced botany exam at the University of Vermont)

The first question in both examples lands with a thud. End of discussion. Good to know, but where does it go? In contrast, the higher-level questions prod students to evaluate and synthesize information into an argument to support their hypothesis. There may be no one correct answer, but the point is to ask test takers to integrate learning.

Questions, if posed at the higher, more challenging levels, can stimulate learning in the following ways:

- They widen thinking.

  Scientists would never get anywhere if all they did was collect facts. Instead, they might ask, "What other uses can we put this drug to? Why does the Pacific Northwest have an inordinate number of cases of multiple sclerosis? How can we colonize Mars?" All these questions set the stage for further inquiry, and yet more questions.
- They clarify thoughts.

  Socrates used questions to probe into people's statements and beliefs to uncover hidden assumptions and logic. He was put to death because those in power thought he was corrupting the youth by having them question the status quo. So, don't think questions aren't powerful. They are the very antidote a society needs against muddled thinking and deceptive propaganda.

- They excite curiosity.

Marvin Bartel, who taught critical thinking in his elementary art classes, recounted the story of a child who asked how to make pink paint. He had two choices. He could tell her how to do it, or he could ask, "What do you think?" By choosing the second approach, he allowed the child to hypothesize and experiment. Yes, she may have goofed up the first couple of times. On the other hand, if he had given her the information straightaway, she would have had no opportunity to develop those higher-level processes. Now she will never forget how to make pink because she *owns* that information. This is how a teacher should be. This is an example of ideal teaching. The world needs more Marvin Bartels.

The power of asking higher-level questions is only increased if learners create their own. In the beginning. Their tendency may be to opt for the safer, single-answer, lower-level kind. So, modeling the various types of questions, as with the Goldilocks story in chapter 2, shows them how to challenge their thinking at a more sophisticated level.

## Pairing Low-Level and High-Level Questions

In twos, have students formulate a question or two about the material they just read or a question they still have about the material. Perhaps you could even ask them to write pairs of questions: One lower and one higher level. For instance, a lower-level question could be, Who was Little Red Riding Hood? And a paired higher-level question might be, Why do you think Little Red Riding Hood was not scared of the wolf when she first met him in the forest on her way to her grandmother's house? The questions can be posted on the board for discussion.

## Peer Questioning

After presenting a unit about the various methods of saving avalanche victims, have pairs formulate two to three questions to request clarification of a hazy or troubling aspect of the information, or comment on an interesting fact so far. For instance, they might ask their partner,

- What is the length of time a person can stay alive while buried under snow?
- What percentage of people in avalanches are saved? or
- What were the two ways that people can avoid getting trapped by an avalanche?

These questions can be handed in for you to cover in your next lesson. This technique can also be used for large classes, where lecturing can't always be avoided, by giving pairs one minute or so during a natural break in your presentation to ask each other a question. This exercise gives listeners an opportunity to reflect on and absorb the information rather than having only a few ask a question at the end of class.

Another use of peer questioning might come from having them ask about something not yet covered: What kind of equipment do rescuers need to save a victim? How long do they train to become a rescuer? Do they have to already know how to ski at the expert level before entering training? (Take two to three minutes to do this.) Have pairs consolidate/refine their questions, and predict a possible answer. These questions can then be shared with the whole class, who may also hypothesize about the answers or research the answers for the next class session. *Note*: This exercise can also be used at the beginning of a lecture to heighten listeners' curiosity.

## Question Cards (Q-cards)

Hand out blank cards. After introducing an idea or theory or process (perhaps at the end of the class), ask participants to record one thing they learned so far and one thing they have a question about. Allowing learners to ask these in writing gives them a face-saving way to get answers without having to broadcast their ignorance. It also serves to help presenters measure students' understanding and address their concerns right away.

## Questioning Authority

Questioning authority can be intimidating since many cultures teach learners that the professor is all-knowing and someone to revere and sometimes fear. Moreover, asking questions is forbidden because doing so is perceived as challenging the instructor's expertise and is a sign of disrespect. Teachers lecture; students listen. Period. In fact, this is how the To the Moon! exercise (Appendix 2) came about: To help them feel comfortable with asking questions and suggesting possible responses. In other words, they actively participate in the learning process.

The following exercise is another way to help them (gently) straddle an issue and weigh arguments both for and against the question at hand, even if it was put forth by a highly respected authority or political figure.

Have them find an assertion by an author or by some widely respected authority figure, such as NASA saying that Pluto is no longer considered a planet; President Obama saying that legalizing marijuana would be a disaster for the country; your father stating that global warming is a hoax. They can work in small groups to first support that assertion and then provide arguments against.

This is a good exercise to help them see that every controversy has at least two positions and that it's okay, even expected, for them to agree or disagree with it. Examining both sides of an issue, especially those touted by so-called experts, builds a healthy skepticism, and teaches them that ideas, no matter who advances them, should never be swallowed whole. This valuable habit of mind is the only way to sustain a politically diverse and democratic society.

## *"Quickthink"*

Jennifer Moon recommends doing a "quickthink" exercise, wherein students raise a question(s) in small groups or discuss a term or controversial issue for three or four minutes. One group member takes notes of the comments and conclusions, and groups report out to the whole class. (*Note*: This exercise can be used to react to the main idea or portion of a lecture or reading as well.)

To recap this section, questions offer an opportunity to ferret out confusion, extend thinking, and keep listeners actively engaged in the topic by formulating questions that don't have just one answer. Clearly, questions serve a useful purpose well beyond merely testing knowledge at the end of instruction.

## Writing and Critical Thinking

Writing is a jewel in the crown when it comes to critical thinking aids because the very process of putting words on paper can accomplish many tasks. First, writing helps you find out what you're thinking. Free writing, even for just five minutes on a topic, often allows hidden thoughts and insights to leak out onto the paper if given a chance. It can actually force writers to make new relationships between previously unrelated pieces of information, thereby helping them come to know more than they did before they wrote about it. Experts call this phenomenon writing to learn. Here's how it works.

Let's say you are teaching a unit on Pablo Neruda's poetry. You could first ask students to freewrite about one of their favorite poems, saying whatever comes to mind about it. Once these general musings are on paper, you can then ask more directed questions, for example, Discuss a word Neruda used in that poem that is ambiguous or metaphorical. What connection is there between this poem and one you really dislike? What emotions did you experience while reading both?

These questions can clarify thinking, integrate ideas, establish relationships, and promote personal involvement with the material. While literature teachers may not be at all surprised by this suggestion, biology teachers may also find this technique fruitful by asking questions such as: "Write about what you learned in yesterday's lesson on mollusks. What kind of mollusk interests you the most? What do you think we will learn today about other invertebrates?"

Last, writing catches lightning in a bottle because human thought happens at astounding speed and can leave ideas unexamined and connections unrealized. Whether freewriting or guided by questions, recording one's thoughts offers a pause button to chew, swallow, and digest information instead of merely inhaling it like an invisible gas. Having learners access their views via writing is the first step. Holding them up to scrutiny is the job of the critical thinker.

On the surface, it may seem that poor writing is a result of poor writing instruction. More probable is that poor writers have never been taught *to think*. And they can learn to do so by means of writing. It doesn't matter which comes first, the thinking or the writing, because both processes work in a dialectical fashion: Writers can see what they are thinking, review, revise, review, revise, until the writing is clear, precise, logical, and so on.

Hence, writing becomes a recursive feedback loop between writing and thinking. If they learn how to approach the task this way, beginning writers soon realize that good writing does not automatically spring onto the page in a highly organized, well-supported essay. Even with experts, writing grows in fits and starts because they backtrack, recast, and reconsider, and after much fussing and fuming, the essay comes to fruition. This process is what beginners have to learn as part of good writing. Tighten the thinking, tighten the writing. Repeat.

Novice writers often beg for a formula to get them through the extreme discomfort of learning to think. But a formula is useless unless the writer understands what the formula captures. Beginning physics students can stare at $E = mc^2$ all they want, but it won't reveal the depth and breadth of its meaning. Similarly, formulas for writing a thesis statement may telescope the theory to a line or two, but it will not generate a well-organized essay unless writers understand what a thesis statement is in the first place. (Please see Burkhalter, 2015, "A Dialectical Approach to Critical Thinking through Writing" for an extended discussion about how one such formula can improve critical thinking.)

In short, a formula for creating a thesis statement can provide a starting point, but others may provide a touchstone to revisit often. This kind of formula isn't a prescription but rather a means to setting up a dialog among all the parts of the essay until the writing meets all necessary rhetorical standards.

Writing is a marvelous tool for stimulating critical thinking in all aspects of learning. Take, for example, how it can be used to process information from a lecture or lesson, prod students to generate text, consider their ideas, and confront one's cherished views fairly so content can be examined, embellished, corrected, reorganized, and so forth. Here are some exercises that help with all these aims.

*Reflections*

One way to use reflections is to engage and focus learners' attention on your class or a text and help them shelve, for the time being, their Facebook friends, arguments with parents, their date last night, a sick child, etc. Volunteers can share, offering a good trigger for discussion. It's also helpful from time to time to let writers have their own thoughts without their voicing or your grading them.

The point is to give them space to listen to their inner musings and to perhaps analyze and synthesize information, just as the To the Moon! workshop participants did. You need not grade them, but do let writers know when you plan to read them. They can help you gage their understanding and thinking and determine if you need to retool your lesson. Here are several exercises involving reflections.

*Debriefing to Focus Students' Attention*

Give your class five minutes at the beginning/end of instruction to reflect on anything they want. Alternatively, you could present directed or evaluative questions such as these:

- What do you remember from today's (or our last) class session?
- What do you think is the most important fact or piece of information presented in this class so far?
- What do you think is the strongest argument in support of the president's immigration policy (or topic of the unit) mentioned so far? After writing down your ideas, ask your neighbor what she or he thinks.
- Write a question/s you have about the material, class, field of study—anything.
- What problem(s) are you still having with this skill/problem/unit?
- What about this assignment made you change your mind about X?

*Debriefing after an Assignment*

Reflections can be quite useful for debriefing after observing a class, medical operation, or ceremony. But they also help readers and writers reflect on the meaning of a book or the process of completing an essay. A good reflection is not merely a narrative but can include emotional reactions or items that confused, startled, or pleased the writer. Pupils could also write a reaction to a comment you wrote on their paper, a chapter in a textbook, a theory, the outcome of their experiment, a haiku, a ruling in court—virtually anything that is pertinent to the current topic. Let writers know if you require a certain length. Two pages, double spaced, is often a good length to shoot for because it allows for the development of insights and not merely superficial remarks.

## Letter to the Teacher

Anonymously, if needed, students can write a letter to you giving reactions to (i.e., analyzing) anything about the class: How it is being conducted, what they are having problems with, and whether they are dissatisfied with their grade—anything that is causing them difficulty (or helping them). For instance, in a course on academic presentations, some requested that more media and outside speakers be used and sought additional exercises on how to project their voice.

## One-Minute Papers

Write a one-minute paper that summarizes what they have just learned in a lecture, unit, or chapter (an idea from mathematician David Bressoud as cited in LaPoint-O'Brien (2013)). It may take more than a minute, especially if pupils speak English as a foreign language. This assignment boasts the advantage of having writers recall, integrate, and comprehend the information presented. One-minute papers can be given at any point in the class and boost retention because students must state it in their own words.

## Extended Writing Project

Quite the opposite from writing one-minute papers is an extended writing project based on Bloom's Taxonomy. The approach can be divided however you see fit. Each part is presented below along with its rationale for improving critical thinking. It works well in a ten-week quarter if you give it in four parts (including the final rewrite) or even more comfortably in a semester-long class. Here are the instructions:

### Paper # 1

The first part of this assignment is one of four you will write for this course, but all four essays will be about the same topic, which you will choose according to your interests and major.

The first assignment is to think of a question you have about a problem or issue in your field (or course you have taken). Write a two- to three-page paper about both sides of the issue. In other words, explain why it is an issue at all. What is the controversy about? What do both sides give as evidence for their viewpoint? For instance, if you are in social services, perhaps there is some controversy about how to reach rural communities with urgent messages or public service announcements. Should taxes of city dwellers be raised to provide two-way radios to inhabitants of remote villages?

If you are involved in, or are an avid fan of, a sport, say, football, you could talk about a controversy over how to deal with concussions, ankle sprains, or pitcher's elbow. If you are in computer engineering, you might discuss various ways of dealing with corporate hacking or computer viruses.

Because the topics are almost endless within any field, your challenge is to find one you are really curious or have a strong opinion about, narrow it, and find enough information about it to present issues on both sides.

Rationale: This paper has writers enter the assignment by first asking a question about their field, describing the issue, and briefly explaining why it is an issue at all. Formulating a question about their chosen field gives them buy-in and helps them actively think about their education.

### *Paper # 2*

Your second essay will expand on this same issue (3–5 pages). But you will research the topic to find more information about it and provide the viewpoints of experts. Be certain to provide facts, anecdotes, statistics, and direct quotations from academic sources. Your audience is someone who knows nothing about your field but is very curious. *You have not yet taken a side on the issue in this paper.* You are merely fleshing out details and providing facts and quotes to explain, not persuading. Please include a references section and use in-text citations.

Rationale: Essay # 2 challenges writers to do academic research to help the reader understand both sides of the problem. Warn them that they may feel strongly about one side or the other and will want to skew the information to favor their view. But their side of the controversy should be undetectable from this essay. This assignment asks them to summarize, support, and amplify the discussion about their issue.

### *Paper # 3*

Your third essay is an expansion of paper # 2 (5–7 pages). It will keep the part you have already written and add another section stating which side you agree with and why. This section should come after you have thoroughly explained both sides of the debate and what experts say about it. You will again cite experts to support your view and include all of them in your references section.

Rationale: Writers must now weigh the support for both sides and state their opinion on the issue on the basis of the criteria they set forth. This paper involves analysis, synthesis, and evaluation of the issue as well as defense of their viewpoint with sufficient evidence.

*Paper # 4*

Your fourth and last essay (6–8 pages) will be a rewrite of your third paper that will repair problems with grammar, organization, transitions, in-text citations, support, and/or reference format.

Rationale: This last paper provides an opportunity to perfect the students' piece after receiving written comments and discussing the questions that they have in a private tutorial. Presumably, the time that elapsed between drafts 3 and 4 will allow it to get "cold" and help improve awareness of errors.

The overall benefit of this assignment accrues to the increasing cognitive difficulty: First a description, then an elaboration of this description following research, and finally advancing the students' opinion that evaluates the evidence and supports their side of the controversy. Meanwhile, the topic remains the same. Since good writing is rewriting (and rethinking), this method is superior to having them compose four separate essays on topics you think up, in which they may have little or no interest, and for which they must gather new information every time.

This assignment means students articulate both sides of the issue, research what experts think, formulate their reasoned opinion, and justify it. By breaking the project into stages, they are able to write more in-depth essays that develop critical thinking than they would have with several other unconnected assignments. A secondary but not unimportant benefit is that there is no possibility for plagiarism since they grow the essay from the ground up.

## Discussions and Group Work

As with the To the Moon! exercise above, participants can also practice various cognitive skills through discussions and group work. They can precede and/or follow written work, but they have the benefit of drawing on their oral skills that are often superior to written ones.

### Rank Ordering

Rank ordering is a skill everyone uses all the time: Which pair of running shoes will last the longest, which university should I attend, which candidate will best improve the economy? They might not deal with anything as dramatic as deciding who should colonize the moon or who deserves an organ transplant, but the process is the same, whether it is rank-ordering objects, terms, or characteristics. They all involve evaluation.

Attorneys have to rank-order potential jury members and evidence, managers have to evaluate employees for yearly reviews, rock climbers must determine which route to the top has the best hand and foot holds, etc. It all starts with determining criteria by which you evaluate and rank-order. Students enjoy generating their own.

NASA's education modules titled "Survival" provide two wonderful exercises for history and science classes. One deals with the essentials needed for the survival of settlers in a Jamestown colony and the second is concerned with astronauts stranded on the moon. Both scenarios ask participants to rank-order 15 items in terms of usefulness. Both require some background knowledge. Pairs can pool knowledge, do the exercise (alone or together), and then report out to the class before checking NASA's own answers and explanations.

In a class focusing on business, the teacher might ask participants to rank-order which habits make an ethical business leader. In a law class, after discussing what causes one piece of evidence to be more probative than another, they might list several kinds of evidence and then rank-order them in terms of their reliability according to a certain scenario. A teacher-training class might have pupils devise and order their own list of the qualities of an outstanding teacher. There is no right or wrong way to rank-order, but learners must be able to justify their answers.

## Socratic Questioning

What discussion about critical thinking would be complete without including Socratic questioning? You don't have to be a law school teacher to use such a powerful method. The goal is to tease out beliefs so they can be better analyzed and synthesized into an integrated whole.

Richard Paul and Linda Elder (2007) list six categories of questions to draw from when conducting a Socratic discussion:

- Asking for clarification: "Could you restate that in other words?"
- Probing assumptions: "What are you assuming?"
- Probing reasons and evidence: "What evidence do you have to support that?"
- Asking about viewpoints or perspective: "Are there any alternatives?"
- Exploring implications and consequences: "What would be the result of that?"
- Evaluating the significance of the question: "Is this an important question?"

Adaptations include the so-called fishbowl exercise. Everyone reads the same text ahead of time. Four pupils are chosen to sit in the middle of the room with the rest of the class encircling them. The four discussants, perhaps guided by questions provided by the teacher, talk about the reading. Another group of four outside the circle is assigned the role of observers and rate the discussants according to a checklist. The remaining pupils take notes following a guide for doing so: How was their analysis, preparation, evidence, and so forth? Each pupil should have a chance to fulfill each role but with a different reading each time.

## SEE-I (State, Exemplify, Elaborate and Illustrate)

Gerald Nosich, a faculty member of the Foundation for Critical Thinking, offers a variation on Socratic questioning with this mnemonic SEE-I. Deceptively simple, Nosich (2011) says this exercise helps students clarify their ideas. Here is how it works:

State: State the problem, the idea, the definition of whatever you are working on.

Elaborate: Explain this in more detail and in your own words.

Exemplify: Provide an example.

Illustrate: Use a metaphor or draw a diagram, anything that can clarify this for listeners.

This activity prods learners to develop their ideas instead of putting forth poorly conceived or unsupported ones. Nosich mentions that one does not have to use all of these steps every time. But they are helpful in pointing out that learners need to be precise and clear, which are mandatory elements of critical thinking. Repeated use of these steps will help them internalize the prompts to encourage sound reasoning when the teacher is not around. In the end, isn't this the point of education?

## Making Inferences

Shari Tishman and her coauthors (1995) present another simple yet clever exercise for teaching how to draw inferences and see patterns, a skill used in fields such as archaeology, anthropology, and history, all of which require analysis of data collected from indirect evidence.

In this exercise, the teacher lists several items found in a garbage bag from the next-door neighbor. Students morph into Sherlock Holmes as they categorize the objects and infer what their neighbor has been up to. For example, they might examine these items:

Empty soup cans
Catalogs
*New York Times* newspaper

Bacon grease
Cat food cans
Discarded packaging for a wig
Receipt for an expensive watch
Pay stub for $3,500 for one month of employment at Seattle University
Coffee grounds
Empty yogurt containers
Empty pain reliever pill bottle
Insurance payment receipt for cancer treatment at a local hospital
Wilted roses

From this one list, four groups inferred very different kinds of neighbors: A dying female teacher working at Seattle University, a thief, an advertising agency worker, and a cat owner.

Useful as an introductory exercise before embarking on research for a paper, it shows they must look for patterns in their findings as well as discard irrelevant items. For attorneys, this is an indispensable skill, since the strength of any court case rests on collecting strong, relevant evidence.

## Case Studies

Case studies provide a trove of opportunities for critical thinking. For example, you could give classmates a scenario whose facts they are already familiar with, say, Little Red Riding Hood and ask whether the wolf should be punished for his deeds, or whether he acted solely out of instinct and should therefore be excused. Supreme Court Case Studies provide lots of chances to write their own opinion and debate them. This kind of exercise provides a clear window into their reasoning, which is easily scored using a rubric (See Table 3.1). (Also see chapter 4 for more ideas on rubrics.)

The rubric, which is a guide that lists the criteria for grading or scoring, does not need to be long or complicated. But it should indicate the strengths and weaknesses of the opinion, such as the one in Table 3.1.

Table 3.1  **Primary Trait Scoring Rubric**

| Trait | 3 Points | 2 Points | 1 Point |
|---|---|---|---|
| Analysis of arguments | | | |
| Evaluation of evidence | | | |
| Soundness of conclusion from the facts | | | |
| TOTAL | | | |

*Responding to Cases Studies—Method 1—Modeling*

Before having students write their own opinion on the case, model how you would reason out your own using familiar material: Should Goldilocks be prosecuted for trespassing or should she be found not guilty because she is a minor? Showing observers how you think through a problem is a powerful teaching tool.

*Responding to Cases Studies—Method 2—Discussion Leaders*

Another excellent but time-intensive way to use case studies, which can also culminate in a written opinion, is to develop a discussion leader project. It primes them for an upcoming guest speaker, seminar, or conference.

First class/hour:

Divide the class into groups of three or four. Each group has a leader, a position that rotates within the group. The trainer reads the case study to the whole class. Next, all the leaders meet after class to prepare three to five questions for use in group discussions the next day.

Second class/hour:

Each of the leaders conducts small-group discussions using these questions. After these discussions, leaders meet again after class to combine notes and create a handout that summarizes the important points from those discussions. When the small groups meet again, another group member— not the leader—will use these notes to conduct a discussion about the case. Homework: all students individually form their own opinion about the case and make notes to discuss the next class period.

Third class/hour:

All small-group members discuss their opinions. Then, groups report out their opinions to the class. For homework (or during class), each person writes up his/her opinion to hand in. Writers are now well versed in the issues because they have discussed them several times and considered various opinions. The task can be made much more difficult by asking them to read and then go directly to writing their opinion without benefit of discussion and considering their opinion with others.

## CONCLUSION AND ADVICE FOR
## TEACHERS AND STUDENTS

This chapter is a distillation of many years of experience and research on how best to teach critical thinking through questioning, writing, and oral discussions. Hardly exhaustive, the exercises provide only models that can be tailored to learners of any age and field.

## Advice to Teachers

- Arrange the classroom so learners can collaborate.
- Make your classroom student centered by making *them* do the work.
- Pose various kinds of open-ended questions or ask them to devise their own.
- Provide ample writing exercises to kindle thinking, memory, and analysis of what is still unclear.
- Stimulate class discussions, but hold their feet to the fire by making them justify their answers.

## Advice to Students

- Strive to listen closely, see both sides, remain nonjudgmental, and be fair-minded.
- Understand that all (worthwhile) learning is challenging. If you are frustrated, it's usually a good sign. It means the wheels are turning.
- Stay engaged, challenge your status quo thinking, explore others' viewpoints, and organize your thinking.

All of these should be enough to keep you busy for the rest of your life.

## Chapter 4

# Assessing Critical Thinking

Consider this question: Should testing methods dictate how you teach? Seems a bit backward, doesn't it? This approach sounds like Procrustes, the mythological Greek blacksmith, who either stretched people or cut off their legs to make them fit the iron bed he'd created. When it comes to testing, it seems more logical and sensible to use effective teaching methods and *then* devise ways to measure learning. Better yet, why not have testing serve a dual purpose—to both measure and enhance critical thinking? And it's not even hard to do.

To accomplish these two goals, you need to create a transparent, focused, easy-to-use, performance-based exercise and an instrument showing whether students have learned the material, where they need to improve, and what they need to do to get a better grade. Below are some items to think about when it comes to assessment to be expanded upon later:

- When to assess: At the beginning, middle, or end of instruction,
- Which format: Oral, written, or online,
- Who assesses: Teacher or student, together or alone,
- Which instruments: Rubric, holistic scoring, self-assessment, and
- What to assess: Essay, presentation, debate performance, play, mock trial, class or group participation, poem, outline of a paper—whatever needs to be checked for understanding or proficiency.

When it comes to critical thinking, true–false and multiple-choice tests may serve to generate numbers for your gradebook, but they don't reflect deep understanding because they measure only the lowest-level cognitive activities of remembering and possibly comprehending. Moreover, they take time away from real learning. It doesn't matter whether a student knows that the Civil War lasted four years or can identify South Sudan as the newest country. It doesn't *mean* anything.

So, let's see how learning and testing can be fast friends when it comes to critical thinking. This chapter unpacks that alliance by discussing how, when, and why you should test, and finally, how these practices contribute to critical thinking. First, though, is a brief discussion of the two different ways of testing.

## FORMATIVE VERSUS SUMMATIVE TESTING

Simply put, formative assessments occur throughout the instructional period, whereas summative tests look back at what a student has accomplished by the end of the course or unit.

*Formative assessments* can consist of:

• Short pop quizzes,
• Journals,
• Impromptu responses to your questions,
• Drafts and revisions of writing,
• Class discussion about a reading or theory, and
• Reflections.

*Summative tests* include:

• Standardized placement and achievement tests (ACT, SAT, TOEFL, LSAT, MCAT, GRE),
• Final exams,
• Presentations, and
• Final papers.

Summative tests generate scores that reveal little about the test takers' understanding of the material and provide no chance to challenge or clarify an answer. Whereas summative tests are a snapshot of a student's knowledge base, formative assessments are a video, whose script can be edited before finalizing production. Both kinds measure learning, but formative assessments have these important advantages:

• You see how they are doing before instruction ends so you can tweak the lesson if they don't understand something.
• They see how they are doing and can retool their thinking and performance.

What's more, in terms of critical thinking, formative assessment helps learners reflect, question, analyze, evaluate, make connections, and summarize information. All these activities encourage them to think deeply about the material, give it context, and construct their understanding *as a result of being tested*. In this way, test taking doubles as a learning tool.

Here are some general rules so learners can glean the most of your critical thinking classroom and tests.

1. Design assessments to maximize "washback."

    Assessment expert H. Douglas Brown (2010) explains washback as any feedback aimed at improving performance and understanding. Using meaningful, transparent instruments that measure progress will maximize useful ways to improve. Washback also entails using assessments that outline conditions for peak performance. The goal is to positively influence the teaching and learning.
2. Use formative assessments liberally.

    To paraphrase Rhett Butler in *Gone with the Wind*, students should be tested, and often, and by someone who knows how. The sooner you give formative assessments for critical thinking, the sooner they (and you) can start getting feedback. How often can you say this about a fill-in-the-blank test?
3. Share results with students as soon as possible.

    By giving feedback right away, students can clarify their misunderstandings and reset their study habits to reach the course objectives.
4. Have students help design the instruments.

    Getting students' input when formulating the assessment tool encourages ownership of, and internalization of, the process. Furthermore, this instrument will make grading 100 percent transparent by allowing learners to fully understand how you arrived at their grade.

Please note: Giving proper formative feedback can be challenging and time-consuming. Take, for example, writing a narrative evaluation of an essay rather than just a letter grade. That said, not all formative assessments have to be long, nor do they have to be graded. Some evaluations can be as broad as a check-plus or check-minus, accompanied by a few comments on what that student did particularly well.

## ASSESSING CRITICAL THINKING

Now that some of the more global issues about testing have been covered, the discussion can turn to assessing critical thinking. When designing instruments to test these skills, you must state outcomes clearly. Do you want them to create a large salad bowl out of cocobolo on the lathe? Publish a one-act play? Bake a soufflé that doesn't fall? Tune a piano to A440 using an equal-tempered scale? Once the outcomes are articulated, you can design activities and assessments around them.

Outcomes state in clear—*measurable*—terms what the student will be able to do at the end of each activity, seminar, or unit. Bloom's Taxonomy can guide you. Let's say you teach law and need to create measurable outcomes for evaluating evidence for a mock trial. Here are six based on each level:

- Define ten words from the vocabulary list pertaining to evidence. (Level 1—Remember),
- Explain what probative values are. (Level 2—Understand),
- Dramatize a scene between an attorney, witness, and judge involving a piece of evidence. (Level 3—Apply),
- Analyze two opposing arguments from a case involving police mishandling of evidence. (Level 4—Analyze),
- Evaluate the pros and cons of the judgment of the Supreme Court about evidence tampering. (Level 5—Evaluate), and
- Formulate questions for your seatmate about the probative value of the DNA evidence in this court case. (Level 6—Create).

Choosing the right verb for what you are testing is not trivial because it:

- Aligns testing with teaching,
- Aims testing at a specific cognitive level, and
- Provides a goal for how to better that skill.

By neglecting to choose a specific verb or skill to be tested, like Longfellow's arrow that fell to the ground he knew not where, you risk not knowing where your instruction landed, and learners have no bull's-eye to focus on. The result? No clue about what went wrong or how to proceed. So, choose your verb(s) wisely.

Once the measurable outcome has been chosen, you can set about designing various formative assessments for critical thinking, keeping these particulars in mind.

## When to Assess: At the Beginning, Middle or End of Instruction

Formative assessments can occur at any time during the class, week, or term. They can even be used as a placement or diagnostic test, done on the spur of the moment, graded or not. Giving unrecorded grades on first drafts of essays takes a lot of pressure off writers. Yet the learning effect is still the same. Students can check their understanding and get another chance to succeed. Meanwhile, you get a bird's-eye view of individual progress.

## Which Format: Oral, Written, or Online

In content classes, groups can first pool their knowledge by discussing a problem; then each student hands in a write-up of the process or answer to the problem. Alternatively, they can first write their answer and then share it with the group, revise their reply, and hand it in.

Several software programs can provide instant feedback for fast and quick formative assessment. Sites such as Socrative (free) and Poll Everywhere (fee-based) are two of many. Participants log on to the website and reply to questions set up ahead of time. Both sites report results in real time and give test takers instant feedback. This format does not lend itself easily to long answers and so may be limited in terms of how well it reflects critical thinking. But it could be used to survey students' understanding of certain terms or concepts. You receive a readout of each student's score. From these results, trainers can either review trouble spots or proceed with the instruction. And it has that added quality of being fun.

## Who Assesses: Teacher or Student, Together or Alone

You can mix and match these approaches. In fact, each kind of informal assessment below can be done any number of ways.

- Give "power" quizzes.

  Present a short quiz (perhaps five items) on an overhead slide (or electronically) that students can answer right after the material is presented. Allow them to confer with a partner and ask you questions.
- Give group quizzes.

  Give a choice between different answers on a short quiz about the material, have them discuss in small groups, and then vote by raising their hands.
- Let students design the quiz for each other.

  Pairs and groups can create a test for one another. Either way, the teacher sees what they (don't) know or are struggling with.
- Have learners devise a midterm question for each other.

  Let pairs work together to develop a question for each other for the midterm or final. This exercise allows each to pursue a tailored path of inquiry about a topic. The paper should be a two- or three-page response after doing the research. A grading rubric can be determined in advance by the teacher or the group.

## Which Instruments: Rubric, Holistic Scoring, Self-Assessment

*Rubric*

A rubric is a chart that assigns a numerical value to a particular level of performance. It breaks down the process into primary traits that describe the components of the assignment, unit, and course, whatever is being examined. For instance, for a persuasive essay, you might choose primary traits such as "organization" and "support for arguments," which are more likely to capture the complexity and quality of their thinking. Each level of every skill is described, so it is very clear to both the grader and the test taker what the criteria are. Additionally, the student can see what needs to be done to improve at each criterion.

Rubrics have every advantage over other ways of assessing critical thinking (or any skill for that matter) *except* that they require the assessor's time and judgment. The tradeoff is that they clarify to both the rater and the learner what traits are important in that assignment and provide a transparent means of assessing.

Table 4.1 presents a rubric useful for evaluating that persuasive essay mentioned above. The number of levels is always negotiable, but the more levels, the more judgments you must make. You could even include grammar and punctuation as a trait. With any skill, it's important to use the same traits for each assignment to maintain consistency.

*Holistic Scoring*

There is a speedier method of grading, a holistic scale, which means less labor on your part. Taking again the idea of a scale, you can still rank these

**Table 4.1   Primary Trait Scoring Rubric Explaining Each Level**

| Trait | 3 Points (Excellent) | 2 Points (Good) | 1 Point (Needs Work) |
|---|---|---|---|
| Analysis of arguments | Arguments are well analyzed and show clear understanding of the issues | Arguments are only partially laid out or some are incomplete | One or more arguments omitted |
| Evaluation of arguments | Evaluation clear and complete | Evaluation only partially complete | Evaluation unclear and confusing |
| Soundness of opinion based on facts | Conclusion very reasonable and logical | Conclusion is somewhat reasonable but is not convincing | Conclusion does not follow from the facts presented. Not convincing. |
| TOTAL | | | |

**Table 4.2   Example of a Holistic Scale**

| Points | Description of Level |
|---|---|
| 5–6 | Essay is convincing and arguments are clearly outlined and defended. |
| 3–4 | Essay is not convincing because the arguments lack full development. |
| 1–2 | Essay is poorly developed and no clear structure or arguments are presented. |

same persuasive papers by providing a general description of the quality of the paper for each level, as shown in Table 4.2.

If the speed of grading is more important than detailed feedback, then holistic grading is more appropriate; it just means less feedback for the writer. Pairs or small groups can also evaluate one another's work using this rubric. Called peer review, it gives them practice in evaluation, helps them internalize the criteria, and relieves you of the burden of grading.

The Hurley and Hurley (2013) prison design exercise (discussed at length in chapter 5) includes two assessment components, one peer review rubric and another holistic rubric to score critical thinking. The authors mention that helpful instructions on using the second rubric, along with a rating form, can be found in Facione and Facione (1994).

*Self-Assessment*

Self-assessment is an essential part of any critical thinking classroom. It has the following benefits:

- Students become better learners when they assess their own learning, strategies, and progress. Remember, critical thinking is thinking about thinking. Self-assessment offers an opportunity to do just this.
- Self-assessment encourages independent learning and increases motivation because students know exactly how and what to improve.
- It also discourages dependence on the teacher for assessment.
- It can help teachers see how students view their own performance and whether it matches their own perceptions.

To accurately self-assess, students must *analyze* their own level of understanding and *evaluate* it, thereby using the very critical thinking skills they need to polish. As with any analysis, their self-evaluation rubric will show (1) what they must know/do to succeed, (2) how they are performing, and (3) how to close the gap. But, as with any rubric, they can properly assess their performance only when they clearly understand the targets.

Experts also recommend that pupils be trained in self-assessment. Some may never have done it before, and this activity may conflict with their view of education and expectations about who holds the power ("What do *I* know? *You're* the teacher."). A bit easier than rubrics are Likert scales asking the self-assessors to rate their understanding from, say, 1 through 5. For instance, participants might rate the following:

I understand the purpose of a thesis statement:

Likert scales can be used before and after a unit or chapter, even immediately after the presentation of an idea or concept. This form of self-evaluation

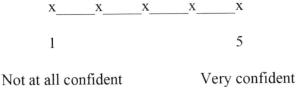

**Figure 4.1    Example of a Likert Scale for Self-assessment**

also reinforces learning because students take responsibility for its assessment. Caveat: As with all self-reports, self-assessments are not necessarily reliable, but they can be used in the spirit of raising consciousness about their understanding. Questions on the Likert scale need not be complicated, but they must ask for a judgment. For example, here are some questions for novice writers:

- I feel confident I can create a focused, narrowed thesis statement.
  1   2   3   4   5
- I know how to cite sources in my essay. 1   2   3   4   5
- I know how to use a semicolon. 1   2   3   4   5

Often new material conflicts with learning in a prior course or reading. This can cause confusion or frustration, even skepticism, over what is being taught. Only through assessment of this new information can they begin to reconcile the conflict between old and new, and assimilate it.

## What to Assess: Essay, Presentation, Debate Performance, Play, Mock trial, Class or Group Participation, Poem, Outline of a Paper—Whatever Needs to Be Checked for Understanding or Proficiency

Anything can be assessed: How well a mechanic fixes a motor, whether an engineer finds a workable solution to cleaning up a flooded area, whether the SCUBA diver performed well on the check-out dive, whether the skydiver packed his parachute correctly, and so on. It doesn't matter what is being assessed, only that it be done with clear, transparent criteria that are provided to the person being evaluated ahead of time.

## CONCLUSION

Assessments can be done anywhere, anytime, in any class. They provide a window into the learning, allowing the teacher to fine-tune instruction. Whether assessment is done alone or in a group, orally or in writing, the point is to keep questions focused on the outcome you have chosen. To scattershot test items is to lose the chance to target further instruction.

Rubrics lend transparency and guidelines for future learning. Likert scales, too, are handy for self-assessment and show learners that they are responsible for their own progress. Rubrics clarify to both instructor *and* pupil what traits are important in the assignment. Any assessment should reflect the outcome(s) of the instruction. Finally, any quiz or test can generate numbers about students' performance, if need be, but their repeated use throughout the instructional time can provide a time-lapse readout of progress as well.

*Chapter 5*

# Teaching Critical Thinking in Other Cultures

It seems pretty obvious that everybody thinks. But not everyone thinks the way *you* think. Even people from your own culture can vary widely in how they approach a problem or learning situation. But if you separate those cultures by oceans and add different schooling, educational policies, languages, religions, and upbringing to the equation, now you're talking vast differences between your cognition and theirs. This chapter outlines those influences, their bearing on critical thinking, and their impact on your classroom.

Chapter 1 began by talking about the differences between Western and Far Eastern thinking. Nisbett presents evidence about variations in attention to and perceptions of objects, drawing causal inferences, organization of knowledge, and reasoning. But his findings are only descriptive and give no insight into how those differences bear on the instruction of critical thinking. Nonetheless, they are an important step toward illustrating that different cultures think differently.

But, there's more to the story. Much more. First, let's consider some general caveats about taking your ideas abroad and then color in some details about how differences in language, thought patterns, and educational background can impinge on your efforts.

## EDUCATIONAL TRANSFER

Going abroad with your information, methods, skills, policies, etc., is called "educational transfer" or "lending." Exchanging ideas is as old as time. But, as many educational lenders have found, once that international border is crossed, it is no longer a matter of simply laying new ideas on top of old, as the term transfer implies. This kind of thinking leads to frustration on everyone's part, not to mention wasting time and money.

The difficulty results from the fact that teaching practices and policies do not travel "in a contextual vacuum or land on a blank slate," as educational transfer expert Iveta Silova (2005) points out, because they are shaped by "historical, political, institutional and structural legacies" (pp. 51–52). Michael Sadler, who studied foreign systems of education over a hundred years ago, said something very similar: Ignore an educational system's deep historical roots at your peril.

> We cannot wander at pleasure among the educational systems of the world, like a child strolling through a garden, and pick off a flower from one bush and some leaves from another, and then expect that if we stick what we have gathered into the soil at home, we shall have a living plant. A national system of Education is a living thing, the outcome of forgotten struggles and difficulties, and of "battles long ago." (as quoted in Beech, 2006, p. 6)

Simply put, you cannot grow an azalea in soil meant for cactus. Should you venture abroad or teach international students within your home country, your first task is to find out what soil you are trying to grow your ideas in and then prepare your plantings (i.e., lessons) specifically for that environment, because you sure as heck aren't going to change the soil.

This information will interest anyone in fields where critical thinking is a necessary component of instruction, such as law, philosophy, science, academic writing, and business. Many believe that taking a course or two in critical thinking will address this issue. However, these efforts would only scratch the surface and ignore many hidden barriers. A word to the wise: These obstacles are real, they are powerful, and they are challenging to address. Ignoring any one of them can stymie your best laid (lesson) plans.

This chapter is divided into three rules: The first outlines problems in teaching nonnative English speakers, the second concerns learning habits, and the third deals with differences in cognition that may result from a punitive educational environment.

## RULES ABOUT LEARNING FOR EDUCATIONAL LENDERS

### RULE # 1: IT TAKES LONGER TO PROCESS MATERIAL, ESPECIALLY NEW CONCEPTS, WHEN PRESENTED IN A FOREIGN LANGUAGE

If you have struggled to learn another tongue, you already know that your mental processing slows down. Just to formulate one sentence with the right vocabulary, correct grammar, proper intonation, and good pronunciation is akin to conducting a symphony orchestra. Talking about simple topics like the weather or your weekend activities lessens that cognitive demand, but even that can be exacting, especially for beginners.

So, when it comes to even more challenging tasks, such as the higher-level thinking skills of analyzing, evaluating, and creating, it's enough to short-circuit all brain function. This is the cognitive load under which all foreign language learners operate. The more fluent, of course, the less significant the demand, but expressing oneself in a foreign language is still a drag on processing.

What follows are some particulars about reading, listening, writing, and speaking in a foreign language and what this means for critical thinkers.

## Reading

Reading presents several challenges for language learners. The first sticking point involves vocabulary and grammar. Do they know enough to be able to extract the meaning of the entire sentence, paragraph, or text? If they can't or if they do it too slowly, critical thinking may also be in jeopardy because it requires an understanding of the entire passage, not just its parts. How can you evaluate the forest when you're focusing only on the trees, or worse, just on the bark?

That forest might consist of determining whether the writer is making assumptions, using irony, putting forth logical arguments, or conveying a certain tone. No metacognition about any of these can happen if readers are stuck on a word or phrase, which in turn means they won't be able to analyze or evaluate the text. And you can forget paraphrasing.

The following paragraph is not in a foreign language, but is written in a way that should challenge your cognitive load in a similar way. Read it once and then try to summarize it.

> Animal testing is necessary because it led scientists discover new medicines, and scientific thouts. The process of developing of finding medicines requires to be experimented on existing genes. Therefore, scientists refer to use around to figure new methods to break a certain diseas. Their testing on animal allow them to find new diseas that do not use to be known at that time, and they developed medicins to its side effects. For instance, a scientist discover diabes diseas while he was traying to develop medicines on mice. Consequently animal testing is necessary to improve medicins and scientic thouts.

You could probably make a wild stab at a summary, thanks to the first and last sentences. But the mind struggles to grasp the overall meaning when attention at the higher level is commandeered to deal with the low-level issues of spelling and grammar. Meaning ends up on a gurney. Now add new concepts into the mix, and there is not a whole lot of learning going on. The cognitive challenge is too great.

## Listening

This same idea of getting the gist is crucial when trying to critically think about what someone is saying. However, with speech, processing the meaning is made exponentially more difficult than reading because listeners cannot control what is being said, nor can they review the utterance. If one's understanding is tripped up by unknown vocabulary or because the lecturer speaks too quickly, then processing is disrupted, and comprehending the whole message becomes a casualty of their inability to keep up. As with reading, little critical thinking can occur when their aural "inbox" gets clogged.

## Writing and Speaking

Writing in another language brings its own cognitive difficulties. All four skills require juggling vocabulary, grammar, and tone, but writing, especially the academic essay, entails a special struggle—organization. Imposing a time limit also greatly increases the processing load and can seriously degrade the written product.

Speaking, like writing, offers more control over the communication because learners never have to process any new vocabulary or grammatical forms. There is no unpredictability to grapple with because nothing they say or write ever goes beyond what they already know. But pressure to make themselves understood in a language appropriate for the occasion can burden them in other ways.

## LEARNING NEW CONCEPTS IN A FOREIGN LANGUAGE

As if all these demands on one's brain weren't enough, there is another aspect to learning that is difficult for anyone, anywhere, any time, and that is new concepts. Take, for example, the notion of thesis statement. Such a term may not even exist in the learner's native tongue, let alone the actual skill to create one. This challenge of processing new concepts in a different language underpins the philosophy of dual-language (aka two-way) immersion classes. This model of learning teaches academic content and literacy in one language and is then reinforced in the target language.

If new and difficult concepts are explained only in the foreign language, they may not be fully grasped because of the twin challenges of processing language and learning the content itself. Just think if you had been taught how to find the value of pi or the process of meiosis in Spanish or Russian. Dual-language immersion dismantles this language barrier in the service of fully grasping the matter at hand.

## SOME ADVICE WHEN TEACHING MATERIAL THROUGH THESE FOUR SKILLS

### When You Speak

- *Slow down, slow down, slow down.* This alone will increase your chances of getting your message across and give listeners time to process.
- Simplify your language by using shorter sentences and less complicated constructions.
- Ask questions periodically to determine understanding.
- Monitor your speech to weed out unfamiliar or high-level vocabulary, slang expressions, allusions, and any culturally loaded material.
- Use signposting liberally, such as "So far, we've been discussing Einstein's theory, which states that. . . . Now let's go on to Stephen Hawking." While this is a good practice in any presentation, it holds true especially for second-language learners.
- Emphasize and reinforce important points by writing them on the board or screen, or by bolding them in text.
- Provide written support material so they can review, highlight, annotate, question, and translate the copy. If you are discussing data that prove global warming is a threat to agriculture, hand out a sheet with the statistics and important vocabulary. Always assume they do not fully understand the information right away. Besides, the more channels they have to absorb the information through, the more solid the learning will be. It also helps audience members to have a printed version of the material so they can easily follow your talk and make notes.
- Summarize key points often, either orally or in writing, or, better yet, have them do it.
- Rephrase questions from students for all to understand what is being asked.

Warning: It can be tiring to constantly monitor your speech, and it takes practice. It's easy to slip back into old speech patterns. Practice makes perfect for you too.

### When Using Simultaneous Interpretation

One way to circumvent all these language issues is to provide simultaneous interpreters. In instances where language skills are too poor for instruction, there may be no option. However, listening through headphones for extended periods exacts its own toll. Sure, it's better than nothing, but it adds to listeners' cognitive load because of the fairly unnatural delivery of speech.

Using a consecutive interpreter has an obvious benefit when it comes to communicating across languages. But consider these challenges:

- It can slow down your presentation by half because you must pause frequently so as not to overload the translator's short-term memory. Speaking in short sentences helps. Writing out an overview of your presentation lets the interpreter research challenging terms and ensures that he or she will adhere to your points.
- Waiting for the interpreter can be quite tedious and disrupt your timing and train of thought.
- It may kill any of those precious teachable moments.
- You may have to devise a way to evaluate students' understanding through their questions and body language with that awkward lag time.

These obstacles may put you off your game at first, but happily, they are all surmountable with practice.

## When Using Texts

Here are some strategies when using written material.

- Budget enough time so readers can absorb the material and confer with others, perhaps even twice as long as you would for native speakers. Think about presenting the material with two goals in mind: First, understanding what the text says, and second, scrutinizing it as critical thinkers. Giving them a vocabulary list ahead of time, perhaps even translated for them, can also aid comprehension.
- Build in enough review. This may be one of the most challenging steps to carry out: It is very easy to think that stating something once means learners will instantly process it or grasp its import. The more complex or new the material, the more time you should allow to dwell on the concept. Remember the Golden Caveat of Teaching: Just because you teach it doesn't mean they learn it.

To review Rule # 1: Learning new concepts in a foreign language increases the cognitive load on a student. When presented orally, it will help to slow down and simplify your speech, grammar, and vocabulary; review and summarize material often; and provide written support for learning. Most important, suppress the fear you are being repetitive. At the very least, repetition allows learners to confirm their understanding.

# RULE # 2: IT TAKES LONGER TO ESTABLISH NEW THOUGHT PATTERNS IN SOMEONE REARED IN A CULTURE WHERE THOSE PRACTICES ARE NOT VALUED OR PRACTICED

## Problem

In Kazakhstan, the master's-level English language teacher trainees had pretty good speaking and listening skills, perhaps a 7 or 8 on a 10-point scale. So, language was not the problem. The new concepts, however, were. Take, for instance, the notion of formative testing. This concept differed 180 degrees from their own testing protocols, which occurred solely at the end of their courses to determine a final grade and only by oral exams. But they balked at accepting the idea. What could be behind this refusal?

Such a conundrum begged for an explanation. An investigation into the Soviet and post-Soviet educational systems shed some light on how these teachers were educated, a process that shaped their habits of learning and teaching practices.

## Background

### Memorization

The emphasis on memorization in the Soviet system cannot be overstated, according to most teacher trainees in Kazakhstan. Long passages from novels were often rewritten from memory, although seldom discussed for themes or ideas. The sheer volume of information students had to memorize was daunting. The aim of Soviet education was to make students feel as if they knew everything about that subject.

In part, this approach was born out of necessity because textbooks for teachers were rare, and even scarcer for students. There simply was no alternative but to memorize. Although several Kazakhstani interviewees said there is still a place for memorization in education, they admitted they had never seen other techniques modeled. They also said it taught them nothing about how to reason with those facts.

### Lecturing

Higher education in both the Soviet and most post-Soviet educational systems consisted (and largely still does consist) mostly of lectures. While excellent for building up a knowledge base, this approach never teaches how to question, synthesize, or evaluate the information. This exact situation was echoed at another Russian university, where graduate and undergraduates reported they had the occasional seminar but were only rarely given opportunities to ask questions, direct their own thinking, formulate hypotheses, or question others' conclusions through debate, reflections, or any other method fostering critical thinking.

Without texts, lecture materials were often written on the board for students to copy. There was no discussion of the lesson with the teacher. Lecturing was such an important aspect of their education that one Kazakhstani student reported that he had had instruction in the theory of giving a lecture! This dull approach to education was intentional because, as Soviet experts Delbert Long and Roberta Long (1999) report, "Inspired teaching could prompt young people to think in unpredictable ways" (p. 102).

## Absence of Independent Thinking

Long and Long also state that schoolchildren learned that there was only one right answer for each question, especially if such matters were important to the state. Teachers were also told to word questions so there would be no doubt about how to answer: "The church claims that it always stood for the defense of the interests of its country and people. Prove that this is not so" (p. 89).

Kazakhstani graduate students in the Teaching English to Speakers of Other Languages (TESOL) program resisted expressing any opinion because they had never done so in their education. What if their observations were wrong, they would fret. Students simply did not trust their own reactions or ideas and waited for the instructor to tell them what to think. Even their thesis topics were given to them.

Often this fear of being wrong led to plagiarizing, an activity encouraged by their teachers. Learners grew accustomed to copying from one another. If that copying was done successfully, it was considered effective cooperation. Other researchers on Soviet education point out that the government suppressed inquiry into opposing views and used the educational system as a means to support its politics. Since citizens were subjected to collective education, it quashed the development of individual and diverse opinions. No wonder plagiarism was (and still is) so prevalent.

## Submission to the Collective

First and foremost, teachers were taught to be teacher-centered, which means they are the source from whom all learning flows, aka the sentry of knowledge, as one teacher trainee put it. They determined the curriculum, readings, and test questions. This orientation was born out of the Soviet tenet that individuals must subordinate their needs to those of the collective. Being individually minded was a "sin," remarks Svetlana Ter-Minasova (2008), a noted and widely published expert in foreign language teaching in Russia.

*Oral Exams*

All interviewees said they rarely took discrete exams, such as multiple-choice or filling in the blanks. Instead, they were graded almost exclusively by oral exams twice a year. All examinees received the same list of 100 questions ahead of exam time, whose answers they memorized. On test day, each pupil in succession took a sheet with three questions on it and recited the answers. The teacher recorded the grade right then and there.

Practices such as memorization, lecturing, adherence to the text, and oral exams are antithetical to the elements of critical thinking: Student-centeredness, active learning, holistic evaluation, and encouragement to question authority. As some educators point out, critical thinking is less likely to emerge in those classes where more emphasis is placed on retrieval of ideas, accuracy of interpretation, test performance, and teacher-sanctioned inquiry.

For students who had never expressed opinions before, never veered from the teaching practices they learned as undergraduates, and learned almost exclusively by rote without analysis or evaluation of the material, there were definitely many hurdles to overcome in a Western-style classroom. All of this militated against adopting strange new practices they neither understood nor respected.

But there was another problem that was difficult to pinpoint at first: They also seemed unusually fearful of, or resistant to, accepting new methods. Rule # 3 addresses the emotional conditioning resulting from their authoritarian education.

## RULE # 3: STUDENTS TRAINED UNDER FEAR MAY RESIST ADOPTING NEW METHODS OR CONCEPTS

So far, rules # 1 and # 2 have discussed difficulties arising from language barriers and learning patterns conditioned by memorization and lecturing that discourage independent thinking. But there is another impediment that may go unnoticed. This obstruction stems from the way individuals were treated as children and students, which in turn influences how they approach future learning. The more rigid and fear-inducing the culture surrounding their upbringing, researchers say, the more likely such learners will see the world through a lens of anxiety and inflexibility, especially when it comes to new ideas.

This special state of mind or attitude is labeled an authoritarian personality. It is a way of reacting to the world that is shaped by harsh, punitive, unbending, dictatorial treatment, whether it be from governments, religion, schools, or families.

Learning conducted in a fear-inducing atmosphere is not easily altered, and the emotional imprinting has the same result: Mental rigidity, closed mindedness, and resistance to change in order to decrease and cope with fear and uncertainty. It is a sort of mental hunkering down to stay safe and maintain control. Unfortunately, such emotional conditioning in childhood bodes poorly for future instruction going beyond their comfort zone. Critical thinking would be anathema to such people since it demands independent thinking and the questioning of authority, to name only two components that clash with the that mind-set.

Outlined below are some of the traits that constitute the authoritarian personality and how each one colors cognition and future learning.

- The tendency to want black-and-white solutions and to arrive at conclusions before they are properly thought out. These people chafe at being in the gray area of indecision and often rush to judgment before all the evidence is presented. Teachers will recognize the "Can't you just tell us the answer?" refrain from students unaccustomed to fully examining an issue or being asked open-ended questions.
- Decreased cognitive complexity. A lessening of ability to perceive nuances and subtle differences. For this group, there is only one answer and no need to discuss how it may differ from other possibilities.
- Uncertainty avoidance. The belief that indecision shows weakness. In contrast, broadcasting certainty shows strength, regardless of whether the decision is half-baked or not even put into the oven. Think about dictators and politicians who need to project power through unwavering conviction.
- Need for cognitive closure. A craving for *any* answer on a given topic that resolves confusion and ambiguity. (See Jost et al., 2003, for more information on the authoritarian personality.)

Those with this authoritarian bent often resist suggestions they should believe something other than what they were taught. Such reactions can be subtle because they are masked by more appropriate behavior. For instance, some will participate, eagerly take notes, and look entirely engaged, but inside they are skeptical and dismissive. Others are easier to spot because they fold their arms, wear a dubious frown, or can even be quite vocal, even rude, in their opposition. Any method other than memorization is not considered "real" teaching.

Rule # 3, then, hopes to alert teachers to this mentality. Some special exercises designed to dodge that mind-set finish out the chapter. First, however, the results of a case study of students educated in several fear-based authoritarian systems describe this behavior in more detail. While this research involves three post-Soviet venues, the effect can be the same on any child exposed to abusive, authoritarian treatment in any culture for stepping outside that group's prescriptions and prohibitions.

## Problem—Resistance

The master's program aimed to impart new methods of teaching English as a foreign language. It was one thing to reject a method they saw as useless, but some showed suspicion of, and even outright defiance toward, adopting others.

Because of their lifelong regimen of knowledge-banking lectures and testing for discrete facts, many protested vociferously against writing reflections about an assignment or activity, complaining reflections were a waste of time and did not further their knowledge of the subject. The ones they did write offered such superficial and general remarks so as to make them useless as a learning tool, for example, "This class taught me about using student-centered teaching." Trainees rarely provided any evaluation of or insight into how they might use these techniques. According to the theory of authoritarian personality, these open-ended assignments were threatening because there was no one correct answer.

A second example of resistance to these new methods manifested when they were asked to collaborate in pairs or groups to confer, pool knowledge, and design mini lessons. They did this begrudgingly, preferring instead to sit benignly and take notes, as they had been trained to do during their school years. After all, what could they learn from someone else who had the same status and level of knowledge as they had?

This resistance was very puzzling to the faculty and was not explained by the causes discussed in Rule # 2. Why would students reject the very techniques they had enrolled in the program to learn? There needed to be a finer point put on the explanation. This nuance was addressed by understanding how punishing the Soviet educational system had been. Only then did it become clear how that treatment hijacked their readiness to adopt new teaching techniques and compromised their cognition.

## Background of the Soviet Educational System

### Using Fear to Control

Very often the literature about the Soviet educational system referred to fear-inducing techniques of humiliation, shame, and overly strict policies to keep everyone under control. For instance, students were ridiculed in front of classmates if they did not prepare well enough. They were expelled if they missed more than three classes. Teachers were closely monitored by administrators who walked up and down the halls, unannounced, to verify whether they were delivering the sanctioned curriculum in appropriate clothing and with students sitting quietly, hands folded on their desks. Any infringement of these rules put their jobs in jeopardy.

Students never asked the lecturer any questions about content because doing so would have implied that the instructor had not provided adequate information or was somehow deficient. The system required complete obedience of students to teachers, and of teachers to the administration.

One of their greatest fears was looking incompetent. As long as they knew the answer, they were safe. That is why open-ended questions or those requiring analysis or hypothesizing frightened them. Students had been conditioned to believe that education is merely consumption of facts and having the "right" answer. Knowing there was only one response helped them avoid uncertainty and the discomfort of ambiguity, and perpetuated the need for cognitive closure. Final oral exams, especially, evoked this fear of looking stupid. Examinees were under such high pressure to perform that some reported feeling nauseated and shook uncontrollably on test days.

With fear blinkering their minds to focus only on facts, the result was intense discomfort over any classroom activity that went outside these familiar practices. That fear meant closing them off to adopting new methods for learning and teaching their own students. Formative assessment was only one such casualty of this fear.

Bob Altemeyer (1988), a noted scholar on the authoritarian personality, explains that people fearful of change and instability are heavily invested in the existing structures of authority and may be quite hostile toward those aiming to change the status quo. Besides, admitting they did not already know something was too shaming. Therefore, any activity encouraging intellectual inquiry and curiosity would have been unnerving to those needing to control their fear, insecurity, anxiety, and uncertainty. For these kinds of people, it was critical to have a belief system that helped them to understand, manage, and reduce these disquieting feelings.

## What This All Means for You

No one can predict how people in or from a foreign country will accept your ideas. But, you *must* be prepared to understand how they have learned in the past and what they expect from you, as educators. To ignore this background means you will have some tough sledding when it comes to asking them to critically think by asking open-ended questions, expressing and supporting opinions, and grasping new concepts. Add to this the onus of doing any of it in a foreign language, and it only increases their fear of looking incompetent.

To be clear, not all learners abroad are resistant, and not all resistant students are overseas. They can be native English speakers reared in an authoritarian family, a strict religion, or a militaristic environment requiring submission to a hierarchy and structure that favors black-and-white thinking and punishes disobedience.

To briefly restate Rule # 3, culture colors cognition. If pupils have been reared in a punitive, authoritarian society, they may have difficulties accepting and using new ideas/concepts brought to them by educational lenders, especially ones that challenge the status quo. Ignoring these differences can thwart even the most skilled educator.

Happily, there are workarounds. Key point: None includes direct confrontation. As with anyone manifesting oppositional behavior (two-year-olds and teens come to mind), such a response will be ineffective and risks provoking disengagement or even anger. While it is true that such a mindset is difficult to change, fruitful solutions may lie in metaphors, distraction, cognitive dissonance, and refocusing their attention on different goals for learning.

## ADVICE FOR EDUCATIONAL LENDERS

### Metaphors

According to George Lakoff and Mark Johnson, authors of *Metaphors We Live By* (2003), metaphors can alter the way you perceive reality by providing a framework for generating new perspectives and approaches. Metaphors bring about this change by providing a bridge to some new idea while hiding certain aspects of the old concept. Thus, metaphors help reorganize ideas and go beyond preconceived concepts and facts to challenge thinking. When dealing with authoritarian students, metaphors can help modify their thoughts without necessarily threatening their identity or triggering fear.

Metaphors don't ask them to abandon beloved teaching methods or to be critical of their past. In short, they are a nonthreatening way to get individuals to at least reconsider their views and beliefs.

As an example, one useful metaphor, comparing learning a language to learning how to ride a bicycle, focused on getting teacher trainees to correct students less when they speak. Constant correction presents unintended problems because doing so short-circuits the speaker's development of fluency and focuses on errors that do not necessarily impede understanding, such as wrong verb tenses and missing articles. More productive is the long-range goal of allowing learners to develop techniques for expressing themselves in novel situations, aka promoting fluency.

To counter this tendency to correct too often, trainees were asked whether they would have the cyclist get off the bike so the teacher could explain correct posture and placement of their feet on the pedals. Their laughter showed they clearly understood the absurdity of such a practice.

(Please note: No language teacher would say that accuracy is unimportant. But error correction should have its own time slot when students can expect correction and can better attend to these issues.)

By using this metaphor, teachers were never directly told their methods were wrong or counterproductive; instead they were gently nudged away from this obsession of constant correction into a different direction by language scrubbed clean of judgment. Metaphors provide an ideal method for examining their own thinking, again privately and without public scrutiny, to honestly consider the arguments and save face in the process.

Since Kazakhstanis pride themselves on their gracious hospitality, it seemed reasonable to tap into this cultural notion to explain the concept of implicit learning, another idea whose premise many students rejected. As second-language learning guru Stephen Krashen (1982) explains, implicit learning means people can acquire a certain portion of the language subconsciously, as opposed to learning it via direct instruction of grammar rules, which Soviet-trained instructors were very fond of teaching, often to the exclusion of many communicative skills. However, because the effects of implicit learning are largely unquantifiable, the trainees regarded it as lazy or no teaching at all. They never trusted anything that could not be measured.

In this metaphor, the trainees were told that implicit teaching was the same as providing a large buffet for language learners with all kinds of food and drink. Their students would be allowed to eat whatever they wanted, but the teachers could not control what or how much they consumed. By refraining from intervening in their students' choices, they were both being hospitable and nourishing their guests, as their culture demands. Because teachers understood—and valued—the concrete custom of eating and setting a fine table, it was much easier to grasp the importance of allowing learners to "graze" at the table of language, even if their learning could not be measured.

Thus, this metaphor portrayed an aspect of teaching in a way that did not confront their loyalty to the grammar-translation model but still conformed to their cultural practices. The metaphor could help them at least *re-evaluate* how it might fit into their teaching.

Metaphors are a versatile, creative, and inexhaustible teaching tool no matter who you are teaching, so it pays to have a repertoire at your disposal, especially when meeting resistance. Nothing is lost by using them, yet there is everything to gain.

## Cognitive Dissonance or Decentering Exercises

Cognitive dissonance is the discomfort individuals feel when they hold two or more contradictory ideas, beliefs, or values at the same time, a loathsome activity for anyone with an authoritarian background. The assignments below employ techniques to shake these hardened beliefs loose using dialectical techniques that oblige them to consider opposing views. It is a good way, as critical thinking teacher John Bean (2011) puts it, to undermine "students' confidence in their own settled beliefs or assumptions" (p. 29).

### Dialoguing with the Enemy

One decentering technique described by Bean asks students to create a dialog between two people on opposite sides of an issue, thus forcing them to communicate with the "enemy" and see something from an unfamiliar perspective. Here is the assignment showing the results from teachers reluctant to adopt a new method of teaching English.

> Write a dialog between two people learning how to teach a foreign language. Bill favors the grammar translation method (translating a document word for word and analyzing the grammar in every sentence) while Mary prefers the communicative approach (focusing on making yourself understood and deemphasizing grammar rules). You are free to write the dialog however you wish, but both characters in their dialog must explain the other's position to ensure they grasp that point of view.

This dialog was written by one student who vehemently opposed the communicative approach.

## THE STUDENT'S DIALOG

**Bill:** People might think that I am old-fashioned but I continue appreciating the grammar-translation method. I think that it has a lot of advantages.

**Mary:** What plusses are you talking about?

**Bill:** The first positive feature of this method is learning grammar rules. When you have finished one grammar rule, only then can you move to another. Students can devote enough time to practicing and drilling each rule so they can understand it better.

**Mary:** But learning the rules does not mean acquiring the language. Look, how many people study the language for decades but cannot speak at all. I prefer the communicative approach when students use all types of grammar at once when they speak.

**Bill:** But then how can you correct students' errors? Do you mean that grammar (accuracy) is not so important for you, and you can allow your students to ignore the important aspects of grammar, such as conditionals or tenses? It is absurd! You can't do this!

**Mary:** Bill, believe me, only when students speak can they activate the language. You can also explain grammar rules in the communicative approach, but it should be done in meaningful context, not in isolation.

**Bill:** Really? Then could you define the communicative approach?

**Mary:** OK. The communicative approach is when students are given a lot of different opportunities to speak, discuss, and practice the language.

Mission accomplished with at least articulating the other side. Whether it changed his mind is not certain. But it provided a low-key, face-saving way to at least exchange ideas with his opponent.

### Classroom Drama

Similar to the written dialog exercise above, orchestrating a classroom drama can slacken an authoritarian student's grip on the "one" truth. It's similar to a debate but is much less formal. It is a staple for psychologists who have clients role-play to see a situation from another's point of view.

In business courses, it could be used to train managers to be on the receiving end of a performance evaluation or be a job applicant. History teachers might set up a drama between Alexander Hamilton and Aaron Burr right before the duel. Science instructors could have Copernicus and Pope Clement VII discussing heliocentrism. In a child development course, Vygotsky might spar with Piaget over stages of cognitive development.

The teacher/facilitator may have to prompt the discussion with phrases or vocabulary, but the point is to have the participants argue and present their side.

### Tetrad

The tetrad is a tool that works for anyone changing a treasured value or practice. Marshall McLuhan (1988) developed it to explain the social processes underlying the adoption of a technology or medium (e.g., radio) by dividing its effects into four categories and displaying them simultaneously. It is easily adapted for use as an exploration of ideas and triggers for thought that might otherwise remain unobserved. As with dual conversations, the tetrad helps students externalize their thinking for more objective analysis. In Figure 5.1, the right side of the tetrad probes negatives aspects of adopting new strategies, while the left side emphasizes the positive ones.

The technique helps learners consider the implications of a new theory, practice, court ruling, technological breakthrough, social policy, university curriculum—any radical shift away from status quo. The more radical, especially for the person experiencing the change, the more this tetrad might help parse feelings more objectively.

Here is an exercise given to teacher trainees asking them about the new ideas they learned about in a teaching methods course.

*The new strategies presented in this course will alter the dynamics in your classroom. Fill in the quadrant below to consider how you might be affected.*

The tetrad could also be used as a brainstorming activity before beginning a persuasive essay on, say, driverless cars. Writers could consider both sides of the ramifications on society or their community of this new technology. For instance,

• Enhance—What/how will driverless cars help what do you do now?

They can help me get to work with less stress because I won't have to worry about traffic jams, road rage, getting directions, and accidents. I can get work done while I am being driven.

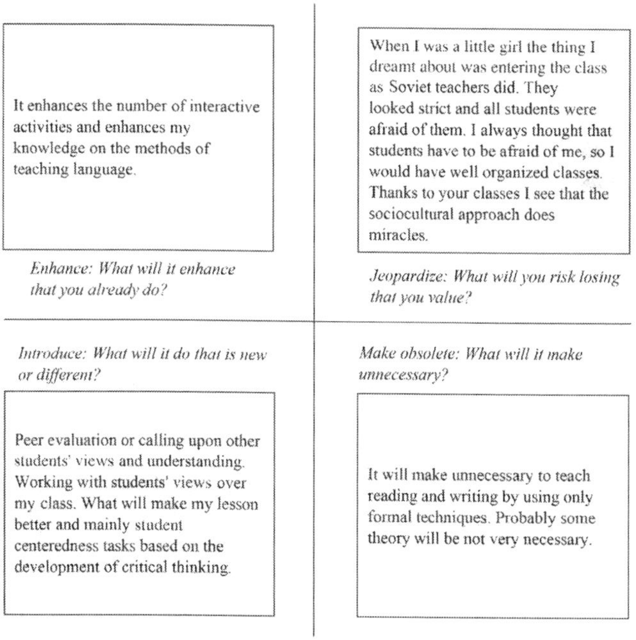

It enhances the number of interactive activities and enhances my knowledge on the methods of teaching language.

When I was a little girl the thing I dreamt about was entering the class as Soviet teachers did. They looked strict and all students were afraid of them. I always thought that students have to be afraid of me, so I would have well organized classes. Thanks to your classes I see that the sociocultural approach does miracles.

*Enhance: What will it enhance that you already do?*

*Jeopardize: What will you risk losing that you value?*

*Introduce: What will it do that is new or different?*

*Make obsolete: What will it make unnecessary?*

Peer evaluation or calling upon other students' views and understanding. Working with students' views over my class. What will make my lesson better and mainly student centeredness tasks based on the development of critical thinking.

It will make unnecessary to teach reading and writing by using only formal techniques. Probably some theory will be not very necessary.

**Figure 5.1 Tetrad**

- Jeopardize—What do you risk losing; what will they reverse?

  I risk being lulled into a false security that the car knows everything. What if the car makes a mistake, such as going down the wrong street? It might not know how to skirt traffic if I am in a hurry by using an alternate route that I might know about but that the car is not programmed to use. What about when a traffic light goes out or someone uses hand signals to direct traffic? How would they know how and where to park? Can it detect black ice and slow down in time?
- Introduce—What is new and different about driverless cars?

  They will introduce a new approach to driving, sort of like having a personal taxi service, and anxiety-free transportation.
- Make obsolete—What will it make unnecessary, or useless; what will be pushed aside or downgraded or ignored?

  They will make driving our own cars obsolete. They will make traffic and speeding tickets obsolete since they will be programmed to go by the speed limit and not go through red lights.

## *Proposing a New Design for a Correctional Facility*

This group activity comes from a very interesting article by Martha H. Hurley and David Hurley (2013) titled "Enhancing Critical Thinking Skills among Authoritarian Students." They teach criminal justice students at The Citadel, a military college in South Carolina. After administering authoritarian personality questionnaires to 64 program enrollees, the data showed that those students were high on the scale of right-wing authoritarianism, leading instructors to conclude that these pupils preferred teaching and testing that focused on the first two levels of Bloom's Taxonomy: Lecturing and right-or-wrong questions rather than the open-ended ones.

As they point out in their article, authoritarian personalities prefer an established order and follow official dictates much more so than others. They cling to the norm and feel threatened if asked to veer from it. They also state that right-wing authoritarianism has been connected with more punitive and prejudicial attitudes, values, and beliefs. They conclude that this rigidity hindered some students' development of critical thinking and kept them from considering alternate views of incarceration other than punishment, such as rehabilitation.

To address this rigidity, the authors asked groups to design a new prison to relieve overcrowding. In their plan, pupils had to stipulate the physical layout of the buildings, types of inmates to be housed, plans for living space, description of the daily routine, and its level of security. They were required to read broadly about prison reform, goals of incarceration, prison design and architecture, and rehabilitation of offenders. To the authors' surprise, all of the final designs showed a distinct change in the students' attitudes away from a facility designed to punish to one more focused on rehabilitation.

Although subject specific, this assignment can easily be adapted to any field to challenge students who resist progressing to higher levels of Bloom's cognitive abilities. For instance, you might ask writers to develop a TV show that has characters with wildly opposing views on social matters (à la *All in the Family*). In a law class, ask students to write (or outline) both sides of an opinion that has just been announced by the Supreme Court (or a lower court) and that might have wide implications for their age group or social class.

## Switching their Focus

Consider creating goals that do not ask people to give up behaviors but reward them for adopting new ones. Teacher trainees resisted mightily participating in conferences or writing articles for publication, largely because they didn't know how. But their involvement in a research laboratory, where they received guidance on how to conduct and publish research, boosted their points on yearly evaluations. This method appealed to their self-interest and showed others they were part of a prestigious academic community. This refocusing turned a system of punishment and confrontation into one of incentives.

In sum, these activities keep you from becoming a threatening authority figure and allow learners the space and time to privately examine thoughts. Moreover, if these exercises are ungraded, it gives them little incentive to resist. Change takes time (understatement), but certain teaching practices and exercises can help you sidestep their resistance so they can think more critically about important issues.

## SUMMARY

When introducing material in a language foreign to your audience, be aware of what concepts are new to them, especially those involving higher-order thinking skills. Then, take into account how students have been taught so you can prepare exercises that invite self-reflection and skirt resistance. Last but surely not least: Expect the unexpected, cognitively and otherwise.

# Afterword

My goal with this book is to stimulate thinking, both yours and your students', regardless of geography, language, or cognition. To this end, I have compressed the last 25 years of experimentation and research into this guidebook for you.

Have I addressed everything involved in teaching, learning, and assessing critical thinking? No, not by a long shot. These matters also need more inquiry:

- Whether and how to incorporate informal or formal logic,
- Whether we should teach critical thinking as a stand-alone course,
- How to teach it across the curriculum,
- Whether it transfers to other domains,
- Which definition should hold sway,
- Whether it is even ethical to teach it to international students,
- If it is more legitimate than other ways of knowing,

and much more.

Will some academics find my approach incomplete since I don't expound on these issues? I think we can count on that. They have spent their careers investigating critical thinking and will bridle at truncating even a smidgeon of nuance and detail.

Some readers might think I have conflated higher-order thinking skills, metacognition, and critical thinking. After consulting many sources, I found overlapping meanings and no daylight between the definitions of higher-order thinking and metacognition, which were often treated as synonyms. This doesn't mean researchers in these fields won't find their own meaningful distinctions among them. It can be said, though, that critical thinking is a more applied, definitive set of skills that can be broken down into components, whereas metacognition and higher-order thinking are more global terms. But all encourage active control over thought.

Probably the most contentious issue arises over Bloom's Taxonomy, which, for some, lacks a sound theoretical explanation for critical thinking. One researcher dismissed the use of these discrete categories because he couldn't achieve interrater reliability with his colleagues when creating activities or questions linked to each level.

But for me, the taxonomy's usefulness does not lie in a strict interpretation of the categories but in its ability to raise awareness of the kinds of cognitive activities. It provides a framework and some language about what critical thinking involves for all teaching professionals and not just for the echo chamber of theorists and researchers.

My aim, then, is to provide a pragmatic guide to navigate what can be stormy waters when teaching critical thinking. Bloom's Taxonomy provides one such map. It is not a perfect tool. But it is a helpful way to explain to anyone not formally schooled in teaching or critical thinking what to aim for, and especially for those who teach international students.

I wanted to write a book for that one person struggling to teach the rules of evidence to undergraduate law students in Almaty, Kazakhstan. Or the ESL teacher in Recife, Brazil, teaching her master's candidates to evaluate data and write their thesis in English. Or the business professor who teaches Japanese MBA students how to write and analyze proposals about patent trolls for their Tokyo-based company. Because I haven't seen that book yet. We sorely need one that blueprints the path for those intrepid souls.

So, no, we are not done perfecting our ideas and practices about critical thinking. But, until then, I say: Critical thinking now!

I assume that experienced instructors will easily dovetail these methods with their current ones. You may even know much about critical thinking already and find some information too elementary. If so, please consult the accompanying annotated resources for more detail. All that said, I hope you have gained some insights into the notion that we all think differently and why. This book is my attempt to provide a heads-up about the kinds of minds you might encounter on your journey and what it means for your classrooms.

And finally, I hope you are poised for the exciting challenge of teaching critical thinking. Your efforts will be richly rewarded, if perhaps unappreciated at first.

Consider this story told by a physics professor at a prestigious American university. He tried mightily to bring critical thinking into his curriculum. One day, he recounted, a student approached him after the final exam. Obviously irritated, the brash student, who incidentally got an A in the course, told him he was the worst professor he had ever had. "You didn't teach me anything," the student said, indignantly. "I had to learn everything myself."

"Bingo," the professor replied.

# *Appendix 1*

# Curriculum for Teaching Persuasive Essays to Elementary School Children

Objectives

1. To teach students what persuasive essays are
2. To motivate students to write persuasive essays
3. To improve their critical thinking skills
4. To identify what makes a good persuasive essay
5. To carry over oral argumentation skills to written
6. To improve writing/editing skills
7. To identify good and bad arguments
8. To write their own substantiated arguments
9. To develop opinions and support them

Day 1

- Talk about how students have tried to persuade others in the past.
- Pretend the students want to get a pet for their classroom.
- Determine what arguments could be used to convince the teacher.
- List them on the board.
- Evaluate arguments (which are more convincing than others).

Day 2

- Bring in newspapers for children.
- Talk about editorials versus factual articles.
- Look at factual versus opinion articles and where they are in the paper.
- List differences between the two.
- Find factual/opinion articles on their own (or in groups, pairs).

Day 3

- Read sample Puppy-Landlord story.
- List arguments and counterarguments on the board.
- Evaluate arguments—which ones are convincing and why.
- Map possible new arguments not used in the story.

Day 4

- Review arguments from the Puppy story the day before.
- Rewrite the story on the board with their suggestions.
- Add supporting information to help convince the reader.
- Let students add their own ideas/arguments.
- Show how to use connectives such as *therefore, because, since.*
- Point out how this essay follows the structure for persuasive texts:

Statement of belief—Usually in first paragraph
    Reason 1—Supports statement of belief
       Supporting ideas—tell more about Reason 1
    Reason 2—Supports statement of believe
       Supporting ideas—tell more about Reason 2
    Reason 3—Supports statement of belief
       Supporting ideas—tell more about Reason 3
(Crowhurst, 1991)

Day 5

- Write their own pet story.

Day 6

- Conference with partners or group.

Day 7

- Edit alone, in pairs, or groups.

Day 8

- Final copy written as a group or individually.

Day 9

- Watch "Assignment: The World" (PBS children's weekly news show).

Topic: Should children be able to choose the public school they attend?

- Discuss facts and background.
- Brainstorm in groups various pro/con arguments about the topic.

Day 10

- Debate ideas in two teams of three each in front of class.
- If possible, write arguments and counterarguments on board.

Day 11

- Write letter individually.

Day 12

- Edit.

Day 13

- Final draft.

Day 14

- Look at second composition about the principal.
- Have pairs or groups list arguments in the story.
- Evaluate them (which are more convincing).

Day 15

- Choose a topic for their own letter to their principal.
- Map topics and arguments alone, in pairs, or in groups.

Day 16

- Write their letter to the principal alone.

Day 17

- Students within one classroom debate the issue (who did not debate before) or read compositions aloud, whichever is more productive.

- Students debate those from other classrooms.
- Evaluate arguments (that are more convincing).

Day 18

- Edit.

Day 19

- Final draft.

Day 20

- Read each other's compositions.

(See Applebee et al., 1990, for information about persuasive writing in elementary school students). The following assignments and sample compositions (that were given the highest rating) are from Fredrick's (1979) Writing Assessment Research Report.

Assignment 1: Write a letter convincing your landlord you should be able to keep a puppy despite the rules.

Sample essay:

Dear Mr. Anderson,

My name is Chris Smith. Please let me keep my puppy. He will do anything you tell him to. I love my puppy and want to keep him. He is the only friend I have. He does not bite or nothing like that. He is the nicest dog in the world. He won't have puppies because it is a boy. I will keep him out of trouble too. We will not let him run after people on the streets. We will not let him dump over the cans. He does not keep people up at night, and he is a good watch dog. You will like him. He will even protect you.

Love, Chris Smith

Assignment 2: Imagine your principal asked for suggestions about how to make things better in your school. Write a letter to your principal telling him/her just one thing you think should be changed, how to bring about the change, and how the school will be improved by it.

Sample essay:

Dear Mr. Hopkins,

Our school needs an air conditioner. It is hard to concentrate on school work with such heat. Sweat drips into my eyes when I work, and my shirt sticks to my back.

I think we could ask the school board for money. Donations should make up for the remainder of the money needed. To get these donations, we could have a carnival, sell candy, and ask each child and teacher to bring a small donation.

I think all students could work much better if they were comfortable and relaxed in a cool climate. I, for one, cannot do my best work. Please consider getting an air conditioner for this school.

Sincerely,
Chris Johnson


Additional assignments to practice persuasive writing.

1. Response from landlord to Chris Smith
2. Reply to landlord again
3. Letter asking principal if 4th graders can buy soda at school
4. Letter to teacher asking for a pet for their classroom
5. Letter about what they would change about the school
6. Listing of how an opinion article in a newspaper differs from a factual one

*Appendix 2*

# Bloom's Taxonomy Action Verbs

*Appendix 2*

**Table A2.1  Bloom's Taxonomy Action Verbs**

| Definitions | Remember | Understand | Apply | Analyze | Evaluate | Create |
|---|---|---|---|---|---|---|
| Bloom's Definition | Remember previously learned information. | Demonstrate an understanding of the facts. | Apply knowledge to actual situations. | Break down objects or ideas into simpler parts and find evidence to support generalizations. | Make and defend judgments on the basis of internal evidence or external criteria. | Compile component ideas into a new whole or propose alternate solutions. |
| Verbs | Arrange | Classify | Apply | Analyze | Appraise | Arrange |
| | Define | Convert | Change | Appraise | Argue | Assemble |
| | Describe | Defend | Choose | Breakdown | Assess | Categorize |
| | Duplicate | Describe | Compute | Calculate | Attach | Collect |
| | Identify | Discuss | Demonstrate | Categorize | Choose | Combine |
| | Label | Distinguish | Discover | Compare | Compare | Comply |
| | List | Estimate | Dramatize | Contrast | Conclude | Compose |
| | Match | Explain | Employ | Criticize | Contrast | Construct |
| | Memorize | Express | Illustrate | Diagram | Defend | Create |
| | Name | Extend | Interpret | Differentiate | Describe | Design |
| | Order | Generalized | Manipulate | Discriminate | Discriminate | Develop |
| | Outline | Give example(s) | Modify | Distinguish | Estimate | Devise |
| | Recognize | Identify | Operate | Examine | Evaluate | Explain |
| | Relate | Indicate | Practice | Experiment | Explain | Formulate |
| | Recall | Infer | Predict | Identify | Judge | Generate |
| | Repeat | Locate | Prepare | Illustrate | Justify | Plan |
| | Reproduce | Paraphrase | Produce | Infer | Interpret | Prepare |
| | Select | Predict | Relate | Model | Relate | Rearrange |
| | State | Recognize | Schedule | Outline | Predict | Reconstruct |
| | | Rewrite | Show | Point out | Rate | Relate |
| | | Review | Sketch | Question | Select | Reorganize |
| | | Select | Solve | Relate | Summarize | Revise |
| | | Summarize | Use | Select | Support | Rewrite |
| | | Translate | Write | Separate | Value | Set up |
| | | | | Subdivide | | Summarize |
| | | | | Test | | Synthesize |
| | | | | | | Tell |
| | | | | | | Write |

*Source:* Adapted from http://www.clemson.edu/assessment/weave/assessmentpractices/referencematerials/documents/Blooms%20Taxonomy%20Action%20Verbs.pdf

*Appendix 3*

# To the Moon! A Launch Pad for Encouraging Reluctant Students to Express Their Opinions

## MOON FACTS

Distance from Earth: 240,000 miles (386242 km).

Temperature: 253 F (123 C) (day); −387 F (−233 C) (night).

Surface appearance:

- Craters (from meteorites bombarding it). Largest is 1,300 miles (2,092 km) across.

- Mountains (actually the rims of the craters) over 10,000 feet (3,048 meters) tall.

Gravity: About six times less than the gravity on Earth.

Air (atmosphere): None—gravity is too weak to hold an atmosphere.

Water: Limited amounts.

Sound: None since there is no air, which is needed to conduct sound. When the Apollo astronauts were out on the moon's surface, they could talk to each other and to mission control only by using the radios in their air-filled helmets.

*Source*: Space facts. Retrieved from http://space-facts.com/the-moon/

## The Assignment

Your country is in a race to colonize the moon. It wants to gain strategic positioning and assert control over its minerals. Your government is sending a team of four volunteers to choose and prepare the site on the moon for future missions. These people must be able to survive the three-day journey to the moon and the return flight. Moreover, they must live in very severe conditions until they establish the first outpost. This process could take several months. Survival is not guaranteed. Which four people would you choose to make up the first team to travel to and colonize Earth's moon? Record your answers in the grid provided.

## Volunteers

- Expert in survival techniques
- Carpenter
- Geology professor
- Nursing student
- Flying instructor and navigator
- Chef
- Computer/communications expert
- Astronaut trainee
- Retired photojournalist
- Doctor
- Mechanical engineer
- Scout

## Volunteer Details

1. Military strategist (49)—retired; expert in developing strategic plans for war.
2. Computer/communications expert (19)—has prison record for theft.
3. Doctor (48)—extensive knowledge in the problems of weightlessness; forced to give up medical license in malpractice suit.
4. Instructor in flying and navigation (27)—has trained on moon shuttle simulation equipment.
5. Astronaut trainee (35)—one year of training; two young children.
6. Mechanical engineer (49)—war hero with shrapnel wounds that cause chronic pain.
7. Geology professor (32)—specialty in lunar atmosphere and terrain; in a wheelchair.
8. Chef (42)—army cook, able to making nutritious food; weak heart but otherwise good physical condition.
9. Photojournalist (51)—retired; will write about, photograph, and keep records of mission.
10. Scout (20)—expert in survival techniques, team building experience, and leadership skills; has elderly, sick parents.

| Grid for Recording responses | | |
|---|---|---|
| *Character* | *Reason(s) You Chose This Person* | *Reason(s) You Rejected This Person* |
| Expert In Survival Techniques | | |
| Computer/Communications Expert | | |
| Doctor | | |
| Instructor In Flying And Navigation | | |
| Astronaut Trainee | | |
| Mechanical Engineer | | |
| Geology Professor | | |
| Chef | | |
| Retired Photojournalist | | |
| Scout | | |

# *Appendix 4*

# Annotated Resources

Atkinson, D. (1997). A critical approach to critical thinking in TESOL. *TESOL Quarterly, 31*(1), 71–94.

The author advances some interesting ideas against teaching critical thinking to nonnative English speakers. (1) Critical thinking is a social practice and an organic part of the culture that teaches it and is therefore not very teachable, (2) it is too reductive and excludes other ways of thinking, (3) critical thinking is a culturally based concept and is therefore not a straightforward method that students can easily absorb, and (4) critical thinking does not appear to transfer across domains, even with native language speakers. So, he concludes, there is no use in teaching it. This is one of very few articles that mention critical thinking as a social practice, or that militate against teaching it to international students.

Bean, John. C. (2011). *Engaging ideas: The professor's guide to integrating writing, critical thinking, and active learning in the classroom* (2nd ed.). San Francisco: Jossey-Bass Publishers.

This book is a practical, accessible, jargon-less, ready-to-use text teeming with exercises and clear explanations about critical thinking and writing. It allays fears of those not schooled in the art of teaching writing and shows how to use it as a tool for learning in any discipline. This is the kind of book that teachers, even experienced ones, reach for often to enrich any course through writing and critical thinking. Bean divides the book into four parts: The first discusses the relationship between reading and writing, the second offers problem-based exercises, part three has more in-depth information about teaching using writing tasks and incorporating critical thinking into the curriculum, and the last section provides tips on how to comment on student writing. Bean understands that not everyone is a writing teacher and that all of you are busy toiling in your own content field. However, spending some time with this book will show how to wield the powerful tool of writing to great advantage.

Brookhart, Susan M. (2010). *How to assess higher-order thinking skills in your classroom.* Alexandria: VA: Association for Supervision & Curriculum Development.

Assessment is every teacher's bugbear. But Susan Brookhart has written a very easy-to-read comprehensive book about assessing critical thinking. She divides it into five categories of assessment: (1) Analysis, evaluation, and creation; (2) Logic and reasoning; (3) Judgment; (4) Problem-solving; and (5) Creativity and creative thinking. She also provides simple yet easily adapted problems for each section, along with various assessment mechanisms such as criteria for assessment rubrics. Aimed at teachers at all levels and fields, it's a good book to get you quickly up to speed on assessing critical thinking in your classroom. She provides five common errors in logic along with examples of poor and good reasoning that are a quick brush-up for you or your students.

Browne, M. Neil, & Keeley, Stuart M. (2014). *Asking the right questions: A guide to critical thinking* (11th ed.). Boston: Pearson.

If you would like to get more into the weeds about critical thinking, Browne and Keeley have written a more traditional book about critical thinking and informal logic, for example, fallacies, assumptions, ambiguities, distorted statistics, evidence, and other elements of reasoning. The authors include information about the ingredients of good writing. Written with humor and clarity, it is valuable because it is a bit less technical than some logic books, and includes several practical exercises along with possible answers. Definitely geared to an advanced level, it has nuggets of information and kinds of questions to ask when prodding students to think more clearly.

Chan, Ho M., & Yan, Hektor K. T. (2008). In Mark Mason (Ed.), *Critical thinking and learning* (pp. 44–64). Malden, MA: Blackwell.

These authors argue against John Nisbett's East-West division, saying he has oversimplified the split in terms of critical thinking. They argue it is incorrect to say that Asians don't have any critical thinking skills; they just approach the tasks differently. But the authors don't shed much light on what that means for teaching.

The Critical Thinking Consortium. Retrieved from http://tc2.ca

One of many, but one of the finest, websites for resource development and professional learning. Skewed toward elementary and middle school students, it is adaptable to secondary and even college classes. It is a Canadian, fee-based site providing lots of curricular ideas and materials (some are free). In addition to the website, its project staff develops digital and print support materials, offers speakers to present at various venues, and provides facilitators to collaborate and follow up with teachers to help them implement the tc2 model, as it is called. The group is also active in obtaining grants across diverse topics and interests: Helping principals implement new educational reforms, adapting the website resources into French, and teaching about archaeological thinking, to name only a few fascinating projects.

Foundation for Critical Thinking. Retrieved from www.criticalthinking.org.

The Foundation for Critical Thinking was started by Richard Paul, a prominent philosopher and writer on critical thinking. He and Linda Elder have developed the foundation into one of the most active and comprehensive forces in the United States today. All publications, workshops, and research are centered on the intellectual standards and elements of reasoning. The faculty conducts an annual, week-long conference and several weekend workshops throughout the year. The Thinker's Guide is a series of 22 booklets, with titles such as *How to Improve Student Learning, the Art of Socratic Questioning, the Art of Asking Essential Questions,* and *How to Detect Media Bias &Propaganda.* The material is a bit repetitive and difficult to implement without special training. It is worth considering their wide range of offerings.

Gula, Robert J. (2002). *Nonsense: A handbook of logical fallacies.* Mount Jackson, VA: Axios Press.

Fallacies are inextricably linked to critical thinking because they help evaluate arguments. Gula has categorized over 170 fallacies into themes such as irrelevance (ad hominem attacks, appeal to force, appeal to ignorance); oversimplification (pigeonholing, begging the question, false dilemma); evasion (the half-truth, domino theory, red herring); and a particularly clear chapter on syllogisms. He provides several examples of each kind of fallacy but no exercises. This is a highly usable, compact (175–page) book, suitable for students or for reference. Gula presents what can be a daunting subject in very digestible prose.

Lee, Debra, Hall, Charles, & Hurley, Marsha. (2007). *American legal English: Using language in legal contexts* (2nd ed.). Ann Arbor: University of Michigan Press.

Both Lee and Hurley are attorneys, but all three authors are ESL teachers and have written a superb book to help nonnative English-speaking law students understand basic legal information and the U.S. legal system. They cover six major areas of law (criminal law, civil procedure, torts, products liability, corporations, and contracts), and provide actual cases and statutes so students can become familiar with legal syntax and special vocabulary. The book ends with a chapter on mock trials. The authors aim to hone students' ability to critically read, synthesize information, and communicate with other legal professionals. The book also offers ample exercises for writing, reading, oral communication, grammar, and culture. Supplemental listening activities can also be purchased. In the hands of an experienced ESL teacher and perhaps also a legal professional, this book advances students' knowledge and vocabulary of the legal system while providing sufficient opportunity to learn about the system and practice thinking within it.

Mason, Mark. (Ed.). (2008). Critical thinking and learning. *Critical thinking and learning* (pp. 1–11). Malden, MA: Blackwell.
Those wanting an overview of some of the issues surrounding critical thinking will like this chapter. Mason also distills many of the aspects that scholars include in their definition into a short list.

Moon, Jennifer. (2008). *Critical thinking: An exploration of theory and practice.* London: Routledge.
Jennifer Moon has written a lot about teaching and learning. This book presents her ideas about the teaching of critical thinking. Half of the book discusses the theory of teaching critical thinking and various ways to approach it. The other half provides various categories of exercises, for example, critical thinking and reading, techniques of arguing, and a focus on logic. Those categories are followed by specific exercises for bringing them alive in the classroom. The book is not as user friendly as others mentioned here, but it does contain some good suggestions for activities for more advanced learners.

Moseley, David, Baumfield, Vivienne, Elliott, Julian, Gregson, Maggie, Higgins, Steven, Miller, Jennifer, & Newton, Douglas. (2005). *Frameworks for thinking: A handbook for teaching and learning.* Cambridge: Cambridge University Press.
If you want a resource that condenses several theories on and approaches to thinking, then this is your book. It presents various frameworks and models for instructional design, productive thinking (where frameworks for Bloom, Paul, Ennis, and others who have weighed in on critical thinking can be found), as well as cognitive structure and development. These include theories such as Piaget's stage model of cognitive development, Gardner's theory of multiple intelligences, Belenky's ideas on women's ways of knowing, and more. *Very* dense and hardly a page turner, it's a tour de force of scholarship in a broad and theoretical field. It's an invaluable resource to compare and contrast various theoretical approaches to cognition.

Nosich, Gerald. (2011). *Learning to think things through* (4th ed.). Boston: Pearson.

Gerald Nosich, a faculty member of the Foundation for Critical Thinking, has written a very readable text grounded in the philosophy of Richard Paul. He shows how the standards and elements of reasoning can be implemented in usable and easy-to-understand exercises. He says it was designed as a guidebook for critical thinking in any field and not as a main text (although he maintains he and others have used it as such). It can easily supplement and enrich students' thinking processes about the content in their field.

Ritchhart, Ron, Church, Mark, & Morrison, Karen. (2011). *Making thinking visible: How to promote engagement, understanding, and independence for all learners*. San Francisco: Jossey-Bass.

The authors provide some examples of elementary and middle school students' work, but exercises are adaptable to any level. They have been designed to create a culture of learning through three different kinds of thinking routines: (1) Introducing and exploring ideas, (2) Synthesizing and organizing information, and (3) Digging deeper into ideas. One such routine, "See-think-wonder," has students observe, express their thoughts, and finally ask broader questions about the issues raised by the exercise. Another is having students write a headline for an activity they just experienced. Teachers new to the ideas of critical thinking will find some good activities. It talks some about Bloom's Taxonomy but does not endorse a lockstep implementation, reasoning that pupils think at all levels. It categorizes routines into procedures, processes, or patterns of action that should be repeated to accomplish the teacher's goals. Authors also provide steps, uses, variations, assessments, and tips for each exercise. These routines are described in the text, and a DVD, sold separately, provides seven videos of teacher demonstrations. (DVD is apparently not included with the Kindle edition.)

Root-Bernstein, Robert. (2003). Problem generation and innovation. In Larisa Shavinina (Ed.), *International handbook on innovation* (pp. 170–179). Oxford: Elsevier Science, Ltd.

Root-Bernstein's chapter in this scholarly book with equally interesting ideas is a classic for people wanting to find out details about how questions further critical thinking. As Root-Bernstein states in his abstract, "This chapter explores how problem definition and evaluation act as catalysts for insight and examines strategies used by successful innovators to generate productive problems." It underscores the idea that the memorization of facts is a dead end.

Ryan, Janette, & Louie, Kam. (2008). False dichotomy? "Western" and "Confucian" concepts of scholarship and learning. In Mark Mason (Ed.), *Critical thinking and learning* (pp. 65–78). Malden, MA: Blackwell.
The authors refute Nisbett's notion that East Asians are "non-logical." They state that there is a discrete difference between their thinking and that of Westerners, and that such stereotypes may hinder teachers' creation of curricula and approaches to teaching.

Supreme Court Case Studies. New York: New York. Glencoe. Retrieved from www.bville.org/tfiles/folder3891/sccs.pdf
This website is a trove of material for teaching legal thinking. Here is a description from the website: "The Supreme Court Case Studies booklet contains 82 reproducible Supreme Court case studies. These cases include landmark decisions in American government that have helped and continue to shape this nation, as well as decisions dealing with current issues in American society. Every case includes background information, the constitutional issue under consideration, the court's decision, and where appropriate, dissenting opinions. Each two-page study requires students to analyze the case and apply critical thinking skills. An answer key is provided in the back of the booklet."

Tishman, Shari, Perkins, David N., & Jay, Eileen. (1995). *The thinking classroom: Learning and teaching in a culture of thinking.* Boston: Allyn & Bacon.
The authors, all involved with Project Zero Institute at Harvard Graduate School of Education when the book was written, is one of the most practical textbooks to help K-12 teachers, and even beyond. It has worn well over its 20-year life and is a text worth referring to often for not only theory but also practical applications to thinking. Its many exercises will add depth to any teacher's portfolio of techniques when teaching critical thinking. The chapters are divided among six dimensions of good thinking: (1) The language of thinking, (2) Thinking dispositions, (3) Mental management (metacognition), (4) Strategic spirit, (5) Higher-order knowledge, and (6) Transfer of knowledge between/among contexts. A lot of exercises and an accessible writing style make this book a good reference for novice as well as seasoned teachers.

# References

Altemeyer, B. (1988). *Enemies of freedom: Understanding right-wing authoritarianism*. San Francisco: Jossey-Bass.

Anderson, L. (Ed.), Krathwohl, D. (Ed.), Airasian, P., Cruikshank, K., Mayer, R., Pintrich, P., Raths, J., & Wittrock, M. (2001). *A taxonomy for learning, teaching, and assessing: A revision of Bloom's Taxonomy of Educational Objectives* (Complete edition). New York: Longman.

Applebee, A.N., Langer, J.A., Jenkins, L.B., Mullis, I.V.S., & Foertsch, M.A. (1990). Learning to write in our nation's schools: Instruction and achievement in 1988 at grades 4, 8, and 12. National Assessment of Educational Progress Princeton: Educational Testing Service. Report No. 19–W–02. Retrieved from ERIC database. (ED 318038).

Bean, J.C. (2011). *Engaging ideas: The professor's guide to integrating writing, critical thinking, and active learning in the classroom* (2nd ed.). San Francisco: Jossey-Bass Publishers.

Beech, J. (2006). The theme of educational transfer in comparative education: A view over time. *Research in Comparative and International Education, 1*(1), 2–13. doi: 10.2304/rcie.2006.1.1.2.

Beyer, B.K. (1987). *Practical strategies for the teaching of thinking*. Boston: Allyn & Bacon.

Bloom, B., Engelhart, M., Furst, E., Hill, W., & Krathwohl, D. (1956). *Taxonomy of educational objectives: The classification of educational goals. Handbook I: Cognitive domain*. New York: David McKay.

Brown, H.D., & Abeywickrama, P. (2010). *Language assessment: Principles and classroom practices* (2nd ed.). White Plains, NY: Pearson Education.

Buck Institute for Education. Retrieved from http://bie.org/object/document/sample_project_design_overview_and_student_learning_guide#

Burkhalter, N. (1995). A Vygotsky-based curriculum for teaching persuasive writing to elementary school children. *Language Arts, 72*(3), 192205.

Burkhalter, N. (2011). To the moon!—A launch pad for encouraging reluctant students to express their opinions. *English Teaching Forum, 49*(4), 30–35.

Burkhalter, N. (2013). Overcoming resistance in post-Soviet teacher trainees in Kazakhstan. *Asian EFL Journal, 15*(2). Retrieved from http://asian-efl-journal.com/6753/quarterly-journal/2013/06/overcoming-resistance-in-post-soviet-teacher-trainees-in-kazakhstan/

Burkhalter, N. (2015). A dialectical approach to critical thinking through writing. *INQUIRY: Critical Thinking Across the Disciplines, 30*(1), 17–23.

Crawford, A., Saul, W., Mathews, S., & MaKinster, J. (2005). *Teaching and learning strategies for the thinking classroom.* Amsterdam: IDEA.

The Critical Thinking Consortium. Retrieved from http://tc2.ca/.

Crowhurst, M. (1991). Interrelationships between reading and writing persuasive discourse. *Research in the Teaching of English, 25*(3), 314–38.

Ennis, R.H. (1962). A concept of critical thinking. *Harvard Educational Review, 32*, 81–111.

Facione, P.A., & Facione, N.C. (1994). Holistic critical thinking scoring rubric. Retrieved from http://www.calstatela.edu/academic/aa/assessment/assessment_tools_resources/rubrics/scoringrubric.pdf

Fredrick, V. (1979). *Writing assessment research report: A national survey.* Madison, WI: Bulletin/Wisconsin Department of Public Instruction.

Freire, P. (2000). *Pedagogy of the oppressed.* New York: Continuum Books.

Goldilocks and the Three Bears. Retrieved from http://courseweb.unt.edu/gmayes/documents/Blooms_Taxonomy.html

Halpern, D. (1993). Assessing the effectiveness of critical thinking instruction. *The Journal of General Education, 50*(4), 270–86.

Hurley, M.H., & Hurley, D. (2013). Enhancing critical thinking skills among authoritarian students. *International Journal of Teaching and Learning in Higher Education, 25*(2), 248–61.

Jost, J.T., Glaser, J., Kruglanski, A.W., & Sulloway, F.J. (2003). Political conservatism as motivated social cognition. *Psychological Bulletin, 129*, 339–75.

Klooster, D. (2001). What is critical thinking? *The Thinking Classroom, 1*(4), 36–40.

Krashen, S. (1982). *Principles and practice in second language acquisition.* Hayward, Calif.: Alemany Press.

Krathwohl, D.R. (2002). A revision of Bloom's Taxonomy: An overview. *Theory Into Practice, 41*(4), 212–18.

Lakoff, G., & Johnson, M. (2003). *Metaphors we live by* (2nd ed.). Chicago: University of Chicago Press.

LaPoint-O'Brien, T. (2013). Action research: The development of critical thinking skills. Retrieved from ERIC database. (ED540359).

Lee, D., Hall, C., & Hurley, M. (2007). *American legal English: Using language in legal contexts* (2nd ed.). Ann Arbor: University of Michigan Press.

Lipman, M. (2003). *Thinking in education* (2nd ed.). Cambridge: Cambridge University Press.

Long, D., & Long, R. (1999). *Education of teachers in Russia.* Santa Barbara: Greenwood Press.

Mason, M. (Ed.). (2008). Critical thinking and learning. *Critical thinking and learning* (pp. 1–11). Malden, MA: Blackwell.

McLuhan, M., & McLuhan, E. (1988). *Laws of media: The new science.* Toronto: University of Toronto Press.

Moon, J. (2008). *Critical thinking: An exploration of theory and practice.* London: Routledge.

Moseley, D., Baumfield, V., Elliot, J., Gregson, M., Higgins, S., Miller, J., & Newton, D. (2005). *Frameworks for thinking: A handbook for teaching and learning.* Cambridge: Cambridge University Press.

NASA. (n.d.). Survival! Exploration: Then and now. Retrieved from www.nasa.gov/pdf/166504main_Survival.pdf

Nisbett, R.E. (2003). *The geography of thought.* New York: Free Press.

Nosich, G. (2011). *Learning to think things through* (4th ed.). Boston: Pearson.

Paul, R.W. (1995). *Critical thinking: How to prepare students for a rapidly changing world.* Santa Rosa, Calif.: The Foundation for Critical Thinking.

Paul, R.W., & Elder, Linda. (2007). *The thinker's guide to the art of Socratic questioning.* Dillon Beach, CA: The Foundation for Critical Thinking.

Paul, R.W., & Elder, Linda. (2012). *Critical thinking: Tools for taking charge of your learning and your life* (3rd ed.). Boston: Pearson.

Poll Everywhere. (n.d.). Retrieved from whttp://www.polleverywhere.com

Silova, I. (2005). Traveling policies: Hijacked in Central Asia. *European Educational Research Journal, 4*(1), 50–59.

Socrative. (n.d.). Retrieved from http://socrative.com/.

Space Facts. Retrieved from http://space-facts.com/the-moon/.

Supreme Court Case Studies. New York: Glencoe. Retrieved from www.bville.org/tfiles/folder3891/sccs.pdf.

Ter-Minasova, S. (2008). *Language, linguistics and life: A view from Russia* (2nd ed.). Moscow: URRS.

Tishman, S., Perkins, D.N., & Jay, E. (1995). *The thinking classroom: Learning and teaching in a culture of thinking.* Boston: Allyn and Bacon.

# Index

# About the Author

**Nancy Burkhalter**, PhD, teaches international students in the English Language and Culture Bridge at Seattle University. She was an associate professor and director of a master's in Teaching English to Speakers of Other Languages program in Almaty, Kazakhstan, where she trained teachers for three years. She also had an English Language Fellowship through the U.S. State Department in St. Petersburg, Russia, training English teachers throughout western Russia and Ukraine. Other teaching venues include Saudi Arabia and (West) Germany, as well as several universities in the United States. She researches and publishes articles about teaching critical thinking, crosscultural educational transfer, and the cognitive processes of writing.

Dr. Burkhalter earned a BA in foreign language teaching and linguistics from Northwestern University, a master's in journalism from Ohio University, a master's in English Language Education from Ohio State University, and a doctorate in educational linguistics from the University of New Mexico. She speaks several foreign languages.

Made in the USA
Lexington, KY
05 January 2018